SUPPORT FOR *MISSION SIMPLE*

"**Mission Simple** *is...elegant. It is not focused on a particular improvement methodology, but rather on a way of thinking about fundamental work systems and the inevitable interactions with key stakeholders along the customers' value chain.*"

Brad Beaird
Vice President Quality & Supply Chain
Enovation Controls

"*Striving for exceptional performance challenges all of us responsible for business organizations.* **Mission Simple: Book 1** *describes this challenge as delivering to customers the most value, in the shortest time, for the lowest cost! Authors Oksa & Wentworth begin to lay out a detailed guide based on key qualitative and quantitative concepts, which are sure to help organizational leaders succeed.*"

George Kerwin
President & CEO
Bellin Health

"*This is a well thought out set of steps for organizations to optimize their operations and tie all aspects of running an efficient high value, and highly reliable enterprise. The stories are very enlightening. I see the application in both service, including health care, and manufacturing.*

Ed Millermaier, MD, MBA, FACP
Chief, Primary Health
Spectrum Health Medical Group

Every CFO in the country is going to champion **Mission Simple** in their organizations. It is the most powerful method of improving bottom-line performance I have ever seen."

Bob Barber
Health Care Consultant
RMK Group

"**Mission Simple** is the first business book we've read that really makes sense to physicians — this book is a must read for physicians seeking to navigate the changing healthcare landscape. The key concepts are extremely relevant to our everyday practice and the material is absorbing, intuitive and accessible. We strongly recommend it."

Thomas Marshall, MD,
Saied Assef, MD
Bellin Anesthesia Associates

"A truly amazing approach to managing a business system. **Mission Simple** is tailor-made for the challenges facing healthcare today — it proves healthcare can deliver high quality care and be competitive and profitable."

Jodie A. Boldrighini
Director
Occupational and
Employee Population Health Solutions
Yale New Haven Health System

"We offer population health programs to support the sustainability of our employer-customer businesses. **Mission Simple** has made it easier for us to sustainably deliver value to our customers. The beauty of **Mission Simple** is that it could also play a key role in contributing sustainability to our customers' businesses."

Randy Van Straten
Vice President
Employer Solutions
Bellin Health

Mission
Simple
Book I

Customer-Supplier
Relationships
and the Universal Business
System Design

Marcus A. Oksa, MS, RCP
Michael D. Wentworth, ASD

Supplier

Alexander
&David

iv

Published by Alexander & David LLC
Alexander & David LLC, 201 Eklund Street, Peshtigo, WI 54157

First published in 2016 by Alexander & David LLC

ISBN 978-0-692-38337-7

For information about special discounts for bulk purchases, please contact Alexander & David LLC at 1-920-238-5114.

Cover design by Michael D. Wentworth
Typeface Book Antigua

Contents

Acknowledgements

We are so blessed to have had the support and assistance of so many talented, hardworking individuals. We are truly humbled by their contributions and are deeply grateful. To all of them, we express our sincere thanks.

- **Beth & Ralph Aschenbrenner**, Owners, U.S. Captioning

- **Jim Ball**, Owner, Square One Marketing

- **Bob Barber**, Health Care Consultant, RMK Group.

- **Brad Beaird**, Vice President Quality & Supply Chain, Enovation Controls.

- **Jodie Boldrighini**, Director, Occupational and Population Health Solutions, Yale New Haven Health System

- **Paul Check** and **Shelly Wolf**, LMG Presses

- **Thom Cody**, President, Pathmakers Inc. and his team Kristin, Jennifer and Kelly.

- **Chris O'Connor**, Executive Vice President and Chief Operating Officer, Yale New Haven Health System

- **Mike Dauplaise**, M&B Global Solutions

- **Michael Dimenstein,** Vice President, Compensation & Benefits, Yale New Haven Health System

- **Mike Feudner**, Technology Project Management Specialist, American Family Insurance

- **Mark Grassman**, Owner, Business Excellence LLC

- **Sherri Habben**, Owner, Team Tree Wellness Collaborative

- **Anne Hale**, Director, System Quality, Bellin Health

- **George Kerwin**, President/CEO, Bellin Health

- **Pete Knox**, Executive Vice President and Chief Learning and Innovation Officer, Bellin Health

- **Thomas Marshall, MD** and **Saied Assef, MD**, Bellin Anesthesia Associates

- **Michael Oksa, Jr.,** Workforce Development Coordinator, Role Model, Supporter

- **Mark B. Russi, MD, MPH,** professor of medicine at the Yale Medical School and Director of Occupational Health Services at Yale-New Haven Hospital.

- **Paul Signorelli**, Improvement Advisor, Bellin Health

- **Paul Steel**, President/CEO, Total Quality Inc.

- **Randy Van Straten**, Vice President, Employer Health Solutions, Bellin Health.

- **Su Miller**, South Central Foundation

And a special thank you to all of our clients who have invested in our work along the pathway of our careers.

Foreword

Based upon available research it is safe to say that the majority of organizational strategies, in every business category around the world, fail to get implemented successfully. The rate of failure in successfully implementing strategy falls in the 60-70% range. As a result, the well-intended mission and vision of organizations of all types and sizes never become realized. The social and economic cost of this business phenomenon is staggering and catastrophic for the world. Why do I say this? Because of the concept of compounding. Failure of strategy execution at these levels translates into lost opportunity, and unrealized improvement and innovation. The world economy suffers. While it may be the single biggest issue facing the world today it goes relatively undetected.

On the other hand, what happens when the odds for successful implementation of strategy change? What would happen if success rates were reversed and 70-80-90% levels of successful strategy implementation were achieved? The incredible power of compounding performs its magic and accelerating results are distinguishable in a relatively short period of time. In a competitive environment market differentiated results are quickly visible.

Of course, the question is whether reversing the odds is even possible. Fortunately the answer is yes. While not easy, it is possible. I wish it were as easy as saying that it is just one thing — if only companies did this one thing better. The solution is more complex and is a combination of cultural, behavioral, structural and relational issues. At the end of the day, a complex set of variables must not only be understood but also aligned in a meaningful way.

In *Mission Simple,* Marcus and Michael pave the path toward breakthrough results in performance by providing a conceptual model that deliberately aligns the variables necessary to successfully execute strategy. Out of the complexity comes clarity through the Universal Business System Design. These are challenging times and the stakes are high for our country and the world. In their work Marcus and Michael provide hope.

A clear path forward toward a different set of results is now possible. I encourage leaders to take the time to understand the powerful framework presented in *Mission Simple.* With understanding comes opportunity. Value creation at unprecedented levels in service as well as manufactory companies is the engine of a more sustainable world; *Mission Simple* starts the engine and enables it to operate at maximum performance.

Enjoy!

Pete Knox
Executive Vice President
Bellin Health System
IHI Senior Fellow
Green Bay, WI
October, 2015

ABOUT PETE KNOX

Pete has been associated with Bellin Health System in Green Bay, Wisconsin in a variety of leadership roles for the past 35 years. Bellin has been on the leading edge of quality for many years and is recognized nationally for superior results. Currently Pete is

Executive Vice President, Chief Learning and Innovation Officer. In this role he is responsible for population health strategies, physician networks, employer strategies, learning and innovation, and execution of strategy.

In addition, he is a consultant for health care and non-health care organizations. He is a Senior Fellow at the Institute for Healthcare Improvement (IHI) and serves on faculty for a number of programs. He is also on the board of trustees for the University of Massachusettes Health System in Worcester. His book titled *The Business of Healthcare* is being used by a number of universities and organizations across the country and he is currently working on a second book *The Strategy Execution Playbook*. Pete is a frequent speaker on strategy, strategy alignment, population health and accountable care in the US and Canada. In addition he serves on the strategic advisory board for HFMA related to the transformation of healthcare from fee for service to value based payment.

Introduction

Over many years, through many experiences, working with many incredible people, I have learned a lot about how business is currently conducted and how it should be conducted. Contrary to what many of us think, business is not about a group of people sitting around in a meeting trying to decide what they should or should not do. Business is about understanding who the customer is, what they want, and how the customer can be successful. The customer must be every business's true north.

It never ceases to amaze me the powerful sustainability of ineffectiveness. What I mean is ineffectiveness seems to have a life of its own; its own pulse, its own vital signs. Yet, from time-to-time, a few fortunate, or maybe even lucky businesses are able to stumble upon the secret to escaping the treadmill and experience some level of success. Their secret? It's simple. Their customer directs what they do.

Twelve years ago I had a vision. I thought that if every business could understand the simple principle, "Your customers are who directs what you do," that more businesses would achieve sustainable success. This concept goes beyond "The Customer is Always Right," and moves toward, "The Customer Knows What They Need." As simple a concept as this is, in practice, businesses continue to put their own self-interests ahead of their customers' needs. It seems that the supplier of products and services tells the customer what they want or what they need, and defy the powerful axiom of using the ears and mouth in their proportion: Listen twice as much as you speak.

Now, you might argue that businesses actually do put the customer first. This would appear true if you've read the volumes of books, and attended the countless seminars on the topic, and buy-in to the rhetoric espoused in so many annual reports and advertising campaigns—but it's a fallacy. I have yet to find more than a handful of businesses that use their Customer as true north and commit to a course featuring a measurable system that delivers consistent results.

The failure to focus on the customer has inhibited many businesses from achieving greatness and limited them to a struggle to maintain mediocrity. Not only have these businesses failed to achieve greatness, but they have ridden to the pinnacle of mediocrity upon the backs of their front line staff. There is a ray of light, though. I have met a few leaders who demonstrate significant compassion for their businesses, constituents, customers and consumers—but they struggled to meet their corporate objectives. In one quarter, their customer satisfaction and business finance measures would be up, but employee morale would be down. And the very next quarter, the bottom line would be up and customer satisfaction would be down.

What seems to be consistent in all of these companies, quarter-over-quarter, is they are always trying to get better employee engagement, or employee satisfaction, or employee buy-in to the programs they have been fronting as the next new, better thing. In response to this, it occurred to me that all businesses have one thing in common: *They want to open the doors the next day.* That, my friends, is called sustainability. And, sustainability can only be achieved through a measurable, systematic approach to improvement.

Improvement, as I have learned, has a great cost; and that cost has to be balanced against quality and satisfaction, internally and externally. So most businesses just go for what they know. These businesses will react to what their greatest trouble is that day, week, quarter, or year. Boards of directors get together and instead of planning for the future, they look forward through their rear view mirror. They believe if they do more of what marginally worked last year, they will somehow magically succeed the next.

"We cannot solve our problems with the same thinking we used when we created them."

— Albert Einstein

I spent a lot of time breaking the issue down into three contributing paradigms:

1. Customer-Supplier Relationships, where most organizations do not have a clearly defined set of measures of who is paying them, who they serve, and who they can make demands of;

2. Decision-Makers and Problem Solvers, which is the distinction of the purpose of any given meeting; and

3. Culture and Risk, where these two components seem to be at odds with one another on a daily basis.

It is our assertion, that when everyone in an organization understands their individual purpose in the business system, how they contribute to the greater cause of opening shop tomorrow, empowered with capable processes, clear instructions, and clear expectations, they will achieve higher performance at a lower level of effort. These three things, in that order:

1. Capable process,

2. Clear instructions, and

3. Clear expectations, will effectively eliminate the need for punitive accountability.

It has troubled me for decades that leadership in virtually every industry hasten to "accountability" as the basis for performance.

I say NO! Accountability is for weak business systems. Carrots and sticks are the tools of ineffective leaders. Build your business on measurements, processes, instructions and expectations and you will be able to go to work tomorrow, the next day, and into perpetuity to fulfill your mission.

In this book you will be introduced to thoughts and theories that may not coincide with what you have learned or experienced in your climb. You will be challenged to have an open mind. You may throw this book across the room at times or call us crazy. However, you will discover that the things in this book are true—and as crazy as they may sound, might just work. You will be challenged to explore things you thought were established, generally accepted business practices, but in fact are built on fallacies.

The difference between Mission Simple and all the other things you have heard in the past, is that our system is sustainable. Your business will not only be revived, but will thrive. After finishing this volume, you will have the opportunity to challenge your thoughts and ours. You will have a deeper understanding of the value of Customer-Supplier Relationships. You will be introduced to concepts you have always felt may be true in the pit of your gut, but were afraid to say, or act upon at the risk of being too far out of the box.

We have rescued businesses from the brink, or what they may have thought at the time was a "dip." You have the talent, knowledge, and desire to be bigger, better, and most important, "open" tomorrow.

Mission Simple: Book I sets us on that journey, together. I hope you will come along and enjoy the ride. It is fascinating what Michael and I have learned over the years. It is amazing what we have been able to achieve. There is no such thing as a bad business, only a bad business system. The Universal Business System Design (UBSD) you will learn about in this book is a very concise, deliberate approach to doing business better. When we understand who is asking for what, and from whom we get the inputs, and who is in control of the objectives, requirements and specifications, we get a better understanding of what we need to do to be successful and sustainable.

It is only then that we can start improving our business to be the best in our market, our region, and our industry. These transformations take time, effort and commitment. But, you can do it. We have seen it time and again. This book will introduce you to things you may or may not agree with, but one thing is for certain—you will be challenged whether or not to accept your current business performance.

Marcus A. Oksa, MS, RCP

Peshtigo, Wisconsin

December, 2015

Part 1
Core Principles

HOW TO READ THIS BOOK

Mission Simple Book I is a unique combination of *methodology* and *implementation*.

In Parts 1 and 2, we present three integrated methodologies:

1. *Mission Simple*

2. *Customer-Supplier Relationships*

3. *Universal Business System Design*

In Parts 3 and 4, we present the blueprints for implementing *Customer-Supplier Relationships* and the *Universal Business System Design (UBSD)*. The introductions to both Part 3 and Part 4 provide in-depth details that are critical to understanding the blueprints. The individual chapters provide narrative work flow and process diagrams to guide you through the complete UBSD.

The overall style of the book is to keep the narrative clean and lean because the methodology is deep and complex. We encourage you to go slow and spend time with each chapter before moving on. Regardless of your opinion of the book, after reading *Mission Simple*, your view of your organization will never be the same.

1
Mission Simple

LET'S BEGIN HERE

"Here's our strategic plan," the company President said sliding the rather hefty document across the desk to me. "We hired the best to guide us through this process and this is the result."

I picked up the document and thumbed through it.

"It took us three months to complete," the President said. "I had everyone participate—my Leadership team, directors, managers—."

"Impressive," I said.

The President thought for a moment and said: "I don't know." He picked up the strategic plan and fanned it in front of me.

"All this—and I still don't know if we're making any real progress."

"Where's the problem?" I asked.

"We're not making any more money!" he exclaimed. "We spent all this money on this strategic plan and we're not improving the bottom line — the one thing we agreed was a top priority."

"How fast are you making money?" I asked.

He looked up, "That's a good question."

"How long is it taking from the time you receive an order until the time you receive cash?" I continued.

"I suppose the speed at which we generate cash is important, but how does that impact the bottom line?" he asked.

"Are you exceeding your Customers' expectations for quality, time or cost?" I probed.

"Sure," he said. "We take great pride in exceeding our Customer's expectations."

"And is that investment improving your bottom line?" I asked.

"That's another good question," he admitted.

"The evidence indicates it is not improving your bottom line," I said. He nodded thoughtfully.

"Let's test this," I said. "Are you delivering the most value — in the shortest time — at the lowest cost?"

He thought for a moment. "I hate to admit it, but I don't know."

"Okay," I said. "How about this one — what is the most important thing that needs to happen tomorrow for your business to be a success?"

"Make money?" he asked.

"You need to *open* for business," I replied. "Everything else obscures this simple truth. What is missing is the 'why' behind all of your actions. Why do I invest here and not here? In order to know the *why* you have to know the *purpose* of a business and then what your specific *objectives* are for the business."

"Makes sense," he admitted. "Why we do something must be connected to a desired result."

"Right!" I said. "Otherwise it's waste."

He thumbed the plan a moment and looked at me: "I'm blaming the plan when I should be blaming the lack of focus."

I nodded. "Most strategic plans don't work because the tough decisions required at the front end were never made. You can't build a solid strategic plan on a foundation of sand. It has to be bedrock."

He lifted the strategic plan. "So this is waste?"

"Perhaps," I replied.

"Great," he sighed. "How do we fix this?"

I took the weighty document, opened it to the Mission/Vision/ Value section and tore out the two pages that contained the MVV. I set the rest of the document aside.

"Let's begin here—," I said.

WHAT IS MISSION SIMPLE?

Mission Simple provides organizations with a highly effective methodology for achieving Performance Excellence[1.1] through *exceptional business performance.*

Exceptional business performance describes the state in which an organization is sustainably delivering the *most value,* in the *shortest time,* for the *lowest cost.*

Mission Simple introduces three *qualitative* core principles (Figure 1.1):

1. *Customer/Supplier Relationships*

2. *Decision-Makers/Problem-Solver*

3. *Culture & Risk*

Mission Simple supports its qualitative core principles with a continuous *quantitative* performance measurement cycle: Measure, Diagnose, Resolve. Mission Simple's unique integration of the *qualitative* and *quantitative* ignites exceptional business performance.

Figure 1.1

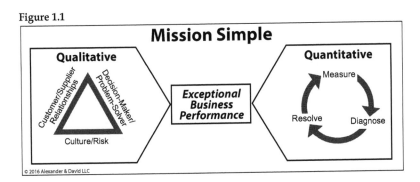

© 2016 Alexander & David LLC

[1.1]Baldrige21.com - The term "performance excellence" refers to an integrated approach to organizational performance management.

Many organizations attempt change and improvement, but sustainable improvement eludes them. They apply new principles but they don't stick. And when they fail to gain traction, the organization discards the principles as ineffective and the organization seeks a new set of principles. This happens because organizations are applying principles only. In order for an organization's investment in business performance improvement principles to deliver sustainable value, there must also be quantitative measurement and quantitative alignment. Mission Simple derives its effectiveness from combining its three core principles with a quantitative Measurement System Design (MSD) and quantitatively aligning the Executive Stakeholders, Customers, Suppliers and the Work System.

CUSTOMER-SUPPLIER RELATIONSHIPS AND THE UBSD

In this book, we will focus on the first principle of Mission Simple: Customer-Supplier Relationships and its framework—the Universal Business System Design (UBSD). Additional books in this series will cover the principles of Decision-Maker/Problem-Solver and Culture & Risk.

We begin with Customer-Supplier Relationships because this principle lays the foundation for the second and third principles; and delivers immediate and significant improvement.

The principle of Customer-Supplier Relationships defines the key *roles* of the business system and the *rules* by which the key roles must work together and support one another. The primary tool that supports Customer-Supplier Relationships is the UBSD.

The UBSD provides the framework to support the principle of Customer-Supplier Relationships. The UBSD defines the relationships and work flow between the key roles in the business system and supports the quantitative alignment between the organization's four core constituents: Executive Stakeholders, Customers, Suppliers and the Work System.

The Mission Simple core principle of Customer-Supplier Relationships is supported by three important methodologies:

1. *Quantitative Alignment*

Quantitative Alignment aligns the organization's four core constituents quantitatively: Executive Stakeholders, Customers, Suppliers and the Work System. Quantitative Alignment eliminates the wide variation associated with *qualitative* alignment and provides the Executive Stakeholders and Customers with a higher degree of assurance that the Work System will meet their objectives.

2. *Managing the Capabilities of Processes*

Managing the Capabilities of Processes shifts the method of achieving business performance results from managing the capabilities of people (wide variation) to managing the capabilities of processes (narrow variation). This approach eliminates the dependence on the exceptional

Figure 1.2:

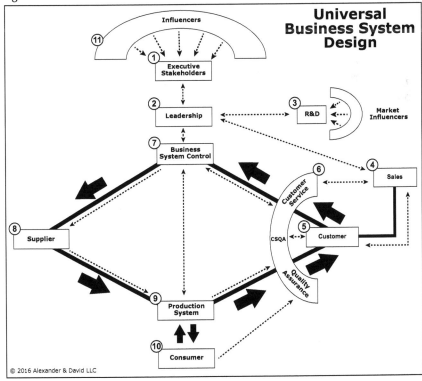

© 2016 Alexander & David LLC

Figure 1.3

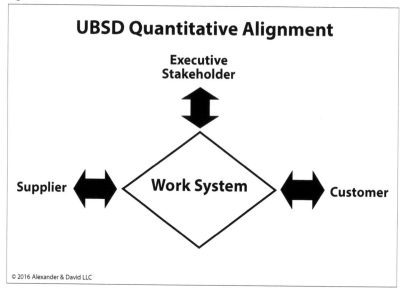

UBSD Quantitative Alignment

Executive
Stakeholder

Supplier   Work System   Customer

© 2016 Alexander & David LLC

few and provides a way for all workers to add more value. Variation is significantly reduced, throughput accelerates, costs go down, margins go up and dependence on the exceptional few to achieve business performance objectives is eliminated.

3. *Measurement System Design (MSD)*

Measurement System Design or the MSD provides a focused, effective approach to measuring and sharing the quantitative data critical to ensuring the effectiveness of the UBSD. It is the engine behind Mission Simple's continuous quantitative performance measurement cycle.

SUMMARY

Exceptional business performance describes the state in which an organization is sustainably delivering the most value, in the shortest time, for the lowest cost. It shouldn't be hard. It should be simple. Our mission is to make it simple for all organizations: *Mission Simple*.

Enjoy your journey.

2
Customer-Supplier Relationships

I CAN'T GET PAST PURCHASING

"You won't believe this," the quality director began. He sipped his Starbuck's dark roast, and sighed deeply. "They assigned me this plant in Illinois. It's an eight-hour drive for crying out loud. I am down there for six months. Back and forth every weekend — and my wife wouldn't let me hear the end of it."

I smiled and nodded.

"They tell me throughput is terrible and we need to improve the overall productivity of the plant," he continued.

He sat back and said: "So I dig in there and, boy, they are drowning in local optimization. You know — everyone optimizing their own little area with no view of the impact they're having on overall throughput."

I sipped my coffee.

"Well — within a month we're already seeing improvement. I mean ten to twenty percent increases in throughput. The plant manager is really excited and we are just getting started."

The quality director shifted in his chair. It was a Saturday and he was dressed in a torn, paint-stained sweatshirt, faded sweatpants and really tired tennis shoes.

"Okay—fast-forward to a month ago," he continued. "The plant manager comes to me and tells me we've got a big problem. So I asked him what it was. He tells me that productivity has improved so much that they are running out of raw materials and parts halfway through the month."

"Interesting," I offered. "Why was that happening?"

"Purchasing is in a different department and that's finance so they report up to the CFO—and not to my boss the COO."

"And why is that a problem?"

"First of the year, the CFO instituted a cost reduction program for the entire company. Purchasing froze spending based on historic averages."

"Before your improvements?" I asked.

"Yup."

"Well—the CFO should be excited by your results."

"You'd think—right? But I can't get past purchasing. I tell them we need more materials and I get 'cost reduction' shoved in my face. So now I have a plant that is sitting idle two weeks a month—and it's already beginning to have a negative impact. The frontline team is stretching out their work times to fill the idle time. They really don't like to be seen sitting around. And they're right—the CFO is going to see this as another opportunity to reduce costs by cutting back the workforce."

"And your COO can't help?"

He shrugged, "It's a board room issue. The CFO and COO have to duke it out and the CEO has to choose. And you know what that means?"

"What?" I inquired.

"The CFO is trump in that card game, baby."

DEFINITION

The rules of Customer-Supplier Relationships,[21] introduced by Toyota's Kaoru Ishikawa, have been widely adopted with proven

[21]*What is Total Quality Control? The Japanese Way*, Kaoru Ishikawa

success. Ishikawa's rules are:

1. *The Customer must provide clear and sufficient requirements to the Supplier; and*

2. *The Supplier must deliver adequate value to meet the requirements of the Customer.*

Mission Simple expands the application of these rules to include the entire business system and the relationships within and throughout the organization. We differentiate the internal relationships from the external relationships in the following way:

> **External** *Customers and Suppliers have big "C" and big "S" when we describe them.*

> **Internal** *customer and suppliers have little "c" and little "s" when we describe them.*

APPLICATION

The framework of the UBSD defines the Customer-Supplier Relationships between the individual Key Work Systems — which role is setting requirements (little "c" customer) and which role is meeting requirements (little "s" supplier).

When these rules are applied to the entire business system, throughput accelerates, waste is reduced, and value is increased. The organization achieves these improvements because the supply being produced by the internal supplier is *quantitatively aligned* with the requirements of the downstream internal customer. This relationship is stable with small variations because it is defined quantitatively by both local and system process capabilities.

IMPACT ON CURRENT STATE

The current state of many organizations features work performed by a key role or Key Work System that is directed and reviewed by a supervisor. The primary impact of Customer-Supplier Relationships on the current state will be the *appearance* of a threat to the Supervisor's authority over their reports. In most current states, Supervisor's direct work. In the Customer-Supplier Relationships model, the Supervisor no longer *directs work*. In the future state, the downstream customer directs work through requirements. Despite this shift, the Supervisor remains critical to the front line team's effectiveness as the Supervisor is responsible for holding the front line workers accountable to following established processes. As we've discussed, a manager can hold a worker accountable to following a process — they cannot hold the worker accountable to the results.

Rather than promoting work team silos and internal competition, the UBSD promotes work teams that support throughput through the adequate delivery of supply across the business system accelerating throughput and eliminating waste.

The UBSD does not eliminate the traditional organizational hierarchy, it makes it more effective. We will explore this shift in structure in more detail in *Chapter 4: Managing the Capabilities of Processes*.

3
The Universal Business System Design (UBSD)

THIS COULD WORK

The phone rang and the department director's eyes turned dark as she laser-beamed her cell-phone. She snatched up the smart phone and swiped the screen: "Yes, Sherry! Right—okay—tell her I'll call her back. Yes—schedule it—great. Thanks!"

She swiped the screen again, checked a couple of texts, thumbed a quick response and sighed, "See what I mean?"

"Why are they calling you?" I asked.

"They have a problem and they need me to solve it," she groaned.

"You're solving problems in the Production System?"

"Of course! Why can't they do it? Are they incompetent or what?"

I considered her situation for a moment, giving her time. This was not the first time I had witnessed this.

"You cannot continue at this pace," I said. "It is unsustainable."

"Right!" she declared and then sighed, "but it's never gonna change."

"I disagree," I countered. "It certainly will change. This pace will lead to decreasing effectiveness, burn out and ultimately a major health issue that will take you down—or you will choose to leave for another job. Regardless of the outcome, it is unsustainable in its current state."

She dropped her face into her hands: "There's nothing I can do."

"That's not true," I said.

She lifted her face and looked at me skeptically.

I asked her: "Why is this happening?"

"I already told you!"

"You're solving problems in the Production System," I responded.

"Right!"

"Why?"

"Because they can't do their jobs!" she cried out.

"Not true," I countered. "They are pulling you into the Production System because that is what they have been trained to do."

"What?"

"In a business system, the number one dysfunction is failure to stay in your position. You charge into someone else's kitchen and create waste."

She gave me a cautious look: "Like what I'm doing?"

"Yes," I said. "But also like what the Production System is doing."

"And?" she prompted.

"The number one reason we leave our position is lack of supply."

"I don't understand," she asked.

"The front line workers are calling you because they are missing supply. What supply are they missing?"

She shrugged, "I don't know. Expertise? Knowledge? Experience?"

"Information," I said.

She wrinkled her brow.

"They have been presented with a request and they lack the instructions telling them how to satisfy the request."

"Well shouldn't they be able to figure it out?"

"That would make them R&D, not the Production System. The Production System must execute and only execute. They are not problem-solvers. You believe they should be problem-solvers because in most organizations, the roles of R&D and the Production System are co-mingled. But in fact, when the Production System solves problems, your throughput slows down and your costs go up."

She considered this for moment.

"Okay—I can see that. But how do we fix it?"

"They need instructions on how to handle every request. Otherwise your phone will never stop ringing."

"But that's impossible."

"Actually, it's simple," I shared. "What they need is a system to cull requests. There are primarily two types of requests, those they can execute and those they cannot. It is the latter type that is creating 'demand waste' in your world."

"Well—who is going to handle the requests they can't handle?"

"A number of roles could—depending on the type of request. The key is to build a system that routes the requests *only* to the role that is capable of executing the request."

She was quiet for moment.

"And this will work?" she asked.

"It will eliminate the phone calls."

"Ha!" she challenged. "I'll believe it when I see it."

"If the Production System has the information they need—the supply they need—why would they call you?"

She considered this for a moment.

"They wouldn't," she smiled. "This could work."

"It does work," I said.

DEFINITION

The Universal Business System Design (UBSD) (Figure 3.1) provides the framework to support the principle of Customer-Supplier

Figure 3.1

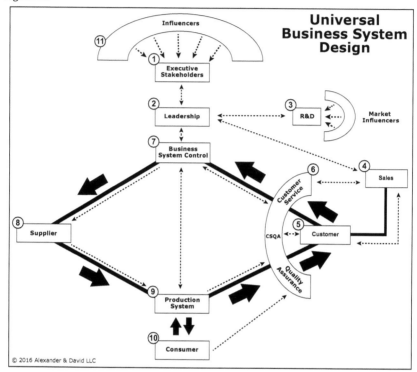

Relationships. The UBSD defines the relationships and work flow between the key roles in the business system and supports the Quantitative Alignment between the organization's four core constituents: Executive Stakeholders, Customers, Suppliers and the Work System.

APPLICATION

The UBSD consists of three core elements (Figure 3.2):

    1. *Key Work Systems*

    2. *Key Work Processes*

    3. *Key UBSD Processes*

1. *Key Work Systems:*

A Key Work System (KWS) is a role in the UBSD that contains one or more value-added processes that transform inputs into

Figure 3.2

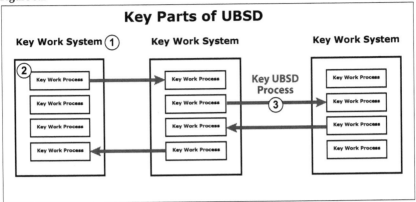

higher value outputs and contribute to the effective delivery of value to the Customer. There are seven KWS's in the UBSD:

1. *Leadership*
2. *Research & Development (R&D)*
3. *Sales*
4. *Customer Service Quality Assurance (CSQA)*
5. *Business System Control (BSC)*
6. *Supplier*
7. *Production System*

3. Key Work Processes:

Within each KWS are one or more Key Work Processes (KWP's). KWP's are "intra" processes and reside solely "within" a single KWS. Collectively, the KWP's produce the output of the KWS.

4. Key UBSD Processes:

Key UBSD Processes (KUP's) are "inter" processes that reside between multiple KWS's linking them to produce specific deliverables of value to the Customer.

THE UBSD ROLES DEFINED:

Executive Stakeholders

The Executive Stakeholders (No. 1 in Figure 3.2) are the organization's owners or owners' representatives (i.e. Board Members and C-Suite executives). They are responsible for making strategic decisions about the Work System; decisions about how to protect and capitalize on the capabilities of the Work System in order to be effective and sustainable in the organization's markets. They are also responsible for making strategic decisions about what should be procured or produced externally to ensure their Work System is effective and sustainable.[3.1]

Leadership

Leadership (No. 2 in Figure 3.2) is the Executive Stakeholder's gateway to the Work System. Leadership is responsible for transforming the Executive Stakeholder's business objectives expressed quantitatively as Key Performance Indicators (KPI's) into quantitative business requirements and then aligning them with the Work System's process capabilities. If the processes are capable of meeting the requirements, then Leadership forwards the business requirements and capable processes to Business System Control, R&D, and Sales. If not, Leadership forwards the business requirements and incapable processes to R&D for redesign. (Note: R&D receives both capable and incapable processes. This occurs because R&D is the only KWS that can redesign its own processes.)

R&D

Research & Development (R&D) (No. 3 in Figure 3.2) transforms incapable processes — the processes that are incapable of meeting the requirements — into capable processes, and designs new processes to meet Customer requirements today and in the future.

Sales

Sales (No. 4 in Figure 3.2) delivers new Customers to CSQA to meet the quantitative business requirements of Leadership.

Customer

The Customer (No. 5 in Figure 3.2) is defined as the payer for a specific value to be delivered by the Work System. The

Customer defines the value they require via quantitative Customer objectives.

CSQA

Customer Service Quality Assurance (CSQA) (No. 6 in Figure 3.2) is the Customer's gateway to the Work System. CSQA is responsible for transforming the Customer's quantitative Customer objectives into quantitative Customer requirements and aligning them with the Work System's process capabilities. If the processes are capable of meeting the Customer's requirements, then CSQA forwards the Customer's requirements and capable processes to Business System Control. If not, CSQA forwards the Customer's requirements and incapable processes to R&D for redesign.

BSC

Business System Control (BSC) (No. 7 in Figure 3.2) transforms the quantitative Customer requirements and the quantitative Leadership business requirements into specifications for the Supplier and the Production System.

Supplier

The Supplier (No. 8 in Figure 3.2) delivers the resources, materials or parts to the Production System to meet BSC specifications.

Production System

The Production System (No. 9 in Figure 3.2) is where the product is produced or the service delivered. It consists of one or more processes that transform supplies and Production System capacity into the value the Customer has requested. The Production System is not always a physical place.

Consumer

The Consumer (No. 10 in Figure 3.2) is the recipient of the product or services being produced by the Production System. The Customer and Consumer can be the same, however, they are not always the same. The difference between the Consumer and the Customer is that the

Customer is always the payer, whereas the Consumer may or may not be a payer — or contributing payer — for the Product or Service.

Influencers

Influencers (No. 11 in Figure 3.2) are independent organizations, non-government organizations (NGO's), social or special interest organizations, or government agencies that impose laws, regulations, or public relations pressure on the Executive Stakeholders in an effort to influence the priorities the Executive Stakeholders set for the organization. In the case of regulatory agencies, they can exert significant influence (e.g. Healthcare, Oil and Gas, Power, etc.) on the organization.

IMPACT ON CURRENT STATE

The business system is not effectively working toward common objectives in the current state of most organizations. For many, the Key Work Systems are co-mingled with weakly defined boundaries. For others, the entire organization is functioning solely in the Production System. These dysfunctional designs create high volumes of waste and threaten the sustainability of organizations.

In Chapter 2, we discussed the weaknesses of the traditional chain of command organizational hierarchy and how they create silos and competitive relationships between work teams. In the current state, the competitive work teams are like roving bands of hunters in search of supply — because lack of adequate supply is the primary reason the work teams leave their positions. Supply is the food they need to survive.

Competitive work teams obtain supply by raiding other Key Work Systems. The result is competitive work teams participate in, and disrupt, multiple Key Work Systems. The volume of waste created in this design is quite remarkable and frequently chokes off virtually all margin from the Work System. The UBSD remedies this.

The UBSD's biggest challenge to the current state will be "establishing trust" that adequate supply will be available. Stephen

M. R. Covey confirmed that: "trust produces speed."[3.2] In the UBSD, trust produces *throughput* speed. All team members must rebuild the trust that has been broken by the silos and competitive work team structure created by the chain of command hierarchy in order for the UBSD to be fully implemented.

[3.2]***The Speed of Trust***, Stephen M. R. Covey (son of Stephen R. Covey, author of *The Seven Habit of Highly Effective People*).

4
Managing Process Capabilities

"Manage the process. Lead the people."

—Marcus A. Oksa, MS, RCP

LOOK, THIS IS NOT EASY WORK

"I don't have enough coders," the manager said.

"Okay," I replied. "How many do you need to fill the order?"

"I need ten," he said.

"And how many are in your Production System?" I asked.

"Well, there are more than two hundred," he responded hesitantly. "But—."

"But?"

"Look—I need *good* ones for this order."

I raised an eyebrow: "*Good* ones?"

"You know—the ones I can really trust. The ones who will always do a great job, never miss a deadline, and the quality is always good," he explained.

"So you don't have to deal with customer complaints—," I nodded.

"Right!" he smiled. "If I use them, I know I won't have to deal with any customer complaints."

"So let me get this straight," I leaned forward and wrote on a yellow pad. "You have two hundred coders, but only a small number of good ones?"

"Right."

"So how many good ones do you have?"

"Oh, I guess twenty to thirty."

"And you only need ten? What's the problem?" I pressed.

"Well, most of them are committed to other projects."

I shook my head in an attempt to achieve clarity. "So how many available good ones do you have?"

"Right now?"

"Yes,—right now."

"None."

I took in a deep breath and slowly let it out as I said a quiet prayer. I began to write on the pad and said: "You have two hundred available coders, but only twenty to thirty are good ones, and you need good ones for this order and, of the twenty to thirty good ones, you have none available?"

"Right."

"Why did you accept the order?"

"We can't turn away business."

I looked at the manager and he could see I was troubled.

He tried to explain: "Look—this is not easy work. There are only a small number of people who are really good at it."

I stared at my pad of paper and considered everything I had heard.

"All right," I began. "You have only ten percent of your resources in the Production System who are really capable of meeting Customer requirements. You can't give the work to the other ninety percent because they don't have the same skill—nor can you give it to the ten percent because they're not available. But you accepted the order anyway because you can't turn away work. Is that the situation?"

"Yup," he smiled. "So how do I fix this?"

I paused for a moment, and then asked: "What are your process capabilities?"

"We really rely on the coders to know what they're supposed to do," he replied.

"If you choose a coder at random from the two hundred and have them follow your process, what is the range of results you could expect?"

"I have no idea."

"Ah!" I raised my pen. "But you do know. You know that for ten percent the results are consistently better than for the other ninety percent."

"Okay — sure — I guess."

"Are they following the same process?" I asked.

"I don't know."

"Do you believe it's the process that makes them better or is it the people?"

"Oh — it's the people for sure."

"But you don't know if they're following the same processes? "

"Ohhhh — I get it," he scratched his chin. "So you think it might be the *way* they do it? I guess that's possible."

"How much more work could you accept if all two hundred were good ones?" I asked.

"Oh — hell — we could double our orders," he said.

"Without adding one dollar of additional cost," I said.

"Right."

DESCRIPTION

Managing the Capabilities of Processes defines the method of achieving business performance results by managing the capabilities of processes — rather than people. This approach eliminates dependence on the exceptional few and provides a way for all workers to add more value.

The purpose of managing the capabilities of processes is to narrow the range of variation such that manual manipulation and *exceptional effort* are no longer required.

> *"CEO's hate variance. It's the enemy. Variance in customer service is bad. Variance in quality is bad. CEO's love processes that are standardized, routinized,*

> *predictable. Stamping out variance makes a complex job a
> bit less complex."*
>
> —Marcus Buckingham

When variation is narrow, throughput accelerates, costs go down, margins go up and dependence on *exceptional effort* to achieve business performance objectives is eliminated. An organization that claims, "only a specific individual can do that," is saying their process has such a wide range of variation, the only way they can trust the results will meet requirements is to have an expert manually manipulate it.

APPLICATION

In order to shift from managing the *capabilities of people* to managing the *capabilities of processes* we must allow the current processes to fail. This requires that the exceptional few—those individuals who are active problem-solvers in the Production System—step back and allow the processes to run without active problem-solving support.

At first, this will appear frightening—especially to managers and Leadership—however, in practice, it rarely jeopardizes Customer relationships and, in fact, more frequently strengthens them.

The process of shifting to managing the capabilities of processes must be managed by a *quality or performance improvement professional* working within R&D. This work must not be managed by anyone in the Work System otherwise the result will be local optimization rather than business system optimization.

The core steps include:

1. *Identify your processes*

2. *Measure to establish process capabilities*

3. *Identify processes with wide variation*

4. *Improve or redesign*

Mission Simple provides three criteria that all processes must meet:

1. **Stable**
   The range of variation is narrow and consistent over time.

2. **Repeatable**
   The range of variation is consistent when the process is performed by the same individual over time.

3. **Reproducible**
   The range of variation is consistent when the process is performed by different individuals over time.

IMPACT ON THE CURRENT STATE

The greatest impact on the current state will be the dramatic reduction of waste and an equally dramatic increase in capacity. This is a good thing, right? Yes, but it will be challenged by those who are participants in the infrastructure of waste.

Managing waste has become the primary job for far too many team members. They perceive their value to the organization is their ability to manage waste. When waste is eliminated, many fear their contribution will no longer be valued—or, worse, their jobs will be eliminated. Both are fallacies. In practice, when waste is eliminated, capacity is increased. Team members are able to shift their focus from managing waste to adding value. The capacity of the business system doubles or triples with little or no increase in fixed costs.

5
Quantitative Alignment

I HAVE NEVER BEEN ASKED THAT QUESTION

"It's all about the relationship," the sales person told me as we walked into the meeting. "Gotta look'em in the eye and shake hands and get to know them."

We were meeting a small healthcare organization.

"They have to know you care about them," the sales person continued.

I nodded.

The meeting followed the pattern of most initial sales meetings. The discussion was primarily *qualitative* — employing subjective words like experience, feelings, perceptions, and wishful terms like wonderful, nice, refreshing.

Despite a spirited, friendly conversation, the meeting itself had not progressed toward a transaction; which, after all, is the objective of all sales meetings.

"If I may," I interjected. "We like to begin our discussions with organizations like yours by *quantifying* what it is you expect to improve or achieve as a result of your investment in our firm."

My sales person was immediately uncomfortable. We had leaped from his comfort zone of undefined *qualitative* value into the world of *quantitative* value. Plus, we had done it with the Human Resources group within a healthcare organization—historically a world defined by *qualitative* attributes.

"Wow," the director replied. "I have never been asked that question."

She thought about it for a minute. Then she said, "That is a really good question. I suppose we want to provide a benefit to our employees."

"For what purpose?" I asked.

The director's associate, a manager, offered: "We have a real problem with turn-over right now. The work we do is stressful. We want to find a way to reduce the turn-over."

"So if you could reduce the turn-over rate, then that would be worth the investment?" I asked.

"Yes!" both the director and manager responded in unison.

"Then let's begin with your historic data on turn-over rates and quantify the cost of your current turn-over rates," I began. "Once we understand the cost, then we will review our process capabilities to determine the improvement our team can deliver and the value in dollars of that improvement."

The director and manager were smiling.

I continued: "Once we have quantified the dollar value of the estimated improvement, then you can judge whether the investment required to achieve the improvement delivers an ROI that meets your risk tolerance."

My sales person was worried. The director and the manager whispered between themselves and then said out loud, "We are very excited about this approach. Our president is a CPA and of course our CFO is a numbers person. They both will really like this approach."

Outside—in the parking lot—my sales person smiled broadly, slapped me on the back and said: "Like I told you, it's all about the relationship!"

DESCRIPTION

Quantitative Alignment aligns the priorities of the Customers and Executive Stakeholders *quantitatively* with the performance of the Suppliers and Work System (Figure 5.1). Quantitative Alignment eliminates the wide variation associated with *qualitative* alignment and provides the Customers and the Executive Stakeholders with a higher degree of assurance that the Work System will meet their objectives.

Qualitative = Wide Variation = High Cost, Low Value

Quantitative = Narrow Variation = Low Cost, High Value

Since the end of World War II, the best minds in science, mathematics, and business have developed effective methodologies for improving the performance of the Work System. However, the Work System is not an independent operation. It exists to serve the needs of the Customer and Executive Stakeholders. This is a

Figure 5.1

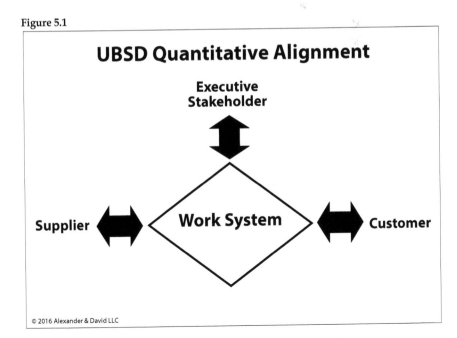

© 2016 Alexander & David LLC

critically important point and we want to emphasize it:

The Work System exists to serve the needs of the Customer and the Executive Stakeholder.

The performance of the Work System must be aligned to the priorities of both the Customer and the Executive Stakeholders.

In the same way, the Supplier's performance needs to align with the priorities of the Work System—rather than the Work System accepting whatever the Supplier is willing to provide. In order for the entire business system to be effective and sustainable, the alignment among these four key players cannot be qualitative; it must be quantitative.

APPLICATION

Mission Simple has established three stages of Quantitative Alignment that connect the Work System Customers (Executive Stakeholders and Customers) and Suppliers (Supplier and Work System) in support of the rules of Customer-Supplier Relationships.

1. **Objectives**

   What we want to accomplish with the help of the Work System.

2. **Requirements**

   The outputs the Work System must produce.

3. **Specifications**

   The resources and capacity required to produce the outputs.

1. **Objectives**

   Only two of the four players in the business system set objectives for the Work System: The Customers and the Executive Stakeholders.

   Customers: *The Customer makes strategic decisions about what should be procured or produced externally to ensure their Work System is effective and sustainable. These decisions are made during strategic planning.*[5.1]

[5.1]Baldridge21.com

Executive Stakeholders: *The Executive Stakeholders are the organization's owners or owner's representatives (i.e. Board Members and C-Suite executives). They are responsible for making strategic decisions about the Work System; decisions about how to protect and capitalize on the capabilities of the Work System in order to be effective and sustainable in the organization's markets. They are also responsible for making strategic decisions about what should be procured or produced internally and externally to ensure their Work System is effective and sustainable. These decisions are made during strategic planning.*[5.2]

The strategic decisions made by the Customers and the Executive Stakeholders are expressed qualitatively as objectives and quantitatively as Key Performance Indicators (KPI's) — a measure used to determine if the Work System is meeting the objectives. KPI's represent the most important metrics for the Work System and, as such, receive the greatest support and funding in the form of investment or budget dollars from the Executive Stakeholders and revenue from the Customers.

2. Requirements

Requirements define the essential outputs of the Work System to meet the objectives. Requirements are defined in terms of quantity, time, quality, and cost.

Requirements identify the Work System processes that must be followed in order to meet the objectives of both the Customers and Executive Stakeholders.

If you know what your processes must produce quantitatively, and you know your process capabilities, you can confidently determine which combination of processes will produce results that meet requirements and objectives.

3. Specifications

Specifications define the Supplier resources, materials or parts, and the Work System process capacity required to meet requirements.

IMPACT ON CURRENT STATE

The impact of Quantitative Alignment is immediate and positive throughout the business system. For the Customers and the Executive Stakeholders, there is now quantifiable confidence their priorities are being met. For the Suppliers and Work System, there is clarity.

6
Measurement System Design (MSD)

QUALITATIVE MEASURES ARE ATTRACTIVE AND TRENDY BUT RARELY HELPFUL

"I just don't understand," the CEO explained. "Our customer loyalty numbers are up, our customer satisfaction numbers are up, our customer experience numbers are up — and we're still not improving the bottom line."

"Do you know which processes improve your customer loyalty measure?" I asked.

He blinked, gave me a look and said: "Uh — well — you know — exceeding the customer's expectations."

"So you have a control chart that shows that when you exceed customer expectations there is a direct correlation to improved customer loyalty?"

"Come on," he said. "This is not quantitative. It's qualitative. It's more *art* than *science*. What was it that Wanamaker said, 'Half the money I spend on advertising is wasted; the trouble is I don't know which half.'[6.1] It's like that."

"Okay, so you're spending more money than you need to— to deliver more value to the customer than they are willing to pay for—and you don't know if that is increasing your customer loyalty—but you think it could be improving it?"

"Yes," he grunted.

"And you don't know why your bottom line is weak?"

He gave me an evil look, "Well—what am I supposed to do? Ignore it?"

"You're measuring *qualitative* measures that may or may not correlate to the investment your making to improve them—and you are not measuring whether or not the improvement in your qualitative measures has any direct correlation to improving your bottom line," I said.

"Ouch," he winced. "Is that as bad as it sounds?"

"Not at all," I assured him. "But you may have been unwittingly misled."

"Really?"

"Qualitative measures are attractive and trendy but rarely helpful—and many times, misleading," I explained. "Many an ad man became wealthy convincing clients that brand recognition mattered. The truth is—it does matter—but not in the way everyone thinks."

"So these measures are misleading?"

"Clearly," I said. "If all of the qualitative measures are positive and yet your primary objective of improving your bottom line is not being achieved—they are meaningless."

"If these qualitative measures are meaningless, then what the hell should I be measuring?" he demanded.

"Let me offer this," I said. "Would you agree that the definition of exceptional performance is delivering the most value, in the shortest time, at the lowest cost?"

"Yes, of course," he agreed.

"Are you delivering the most value?"

"Absolutely. We're exceeding it," he added with pride.

"Are you measuring it?" I asked.

"Uh—no," he admitted.

[6.1]*John Wanamaker* (1838-1922), founder Wanamaker's Department Stores

"So you believe you're exceeding expectations, but you don't know?"

He nodded.

"Okay — are you delivering value in the shortest time possible?"

His head dropped and replied sadly, but honestly: "I don't know."

"At the lowest cost?" I continued.

He looked up slowly, as the light went on: "Probably not. But I don't know."

"So you agree that exceptional performance is defined by quality, speed and cost — and yet you are not measuring those things?"

He was nodding his head now, "Right."

"If you knew those measures, what could you do?" I asked.

He gave me a broad grin, "I'd know how to improve my bottom line."

"Exactly," I said.

DESCRIPTION

Measurement System Design (MSD) defines the engine that drives Quantitative Alignment. The MSD focuses on the most important *quantitative* measures. It provides data collection and distribution processes that keep the entire UBSD aware of the performance status of the Production System.

The MSD replaces subjective *qualitative* measures with objective *quantitative* measures. The weakness of qualitative measures is their subjective nature allows for a wide range of variation. Wide variation creates waste that increases costs, slows throughput and threatens the sustainability of the organization.

To reduce wide variation, the MSD uses quantitative measures to align the priorities of the Customers and Executive Stakeholders with the process capabilities of the Suppliers and the Work System.   Wide variation is reduced when the Suppliers and the Work System invest time and resources *only* in activities that quantitatively impact the objectives of both the Customers and the Executive Stakeholders. In most organizations, more than 50% of time and resources are engaged in activity that does not impact the quantitative objectives of the Executive Stakeholders and the Customers. It is all waste and it is cost that can be eliminated to dramatically improve the organization's bottom line.

APPLICATION

The first step in applying the MSD is to adopt a business system view verses a local process view. Chain of command hierarchy fosters competitive work teams and encourages organizations to focus on *local optimization* rather than *business system optimization*. Improving locally will resolve local problems, but creates waste for other Key Work Systems.

To understand the performance status of a business system, there are only three measures that matter:[6.1]

1. **Throughput** – The rate at which the business system generates cash through the delivery of value in the form of products or services.

2. **Inventory** – The materials that have been paid for but have not yet been sold.

3. **Operational Expenses** – All of the cash spent by the business system in order to turn inventory into purchased products or services.

When you examine these three measures, you will notice they are all *quantitative* measures. Mission Simple has transformed these core measures into an MSD structure called the Simple Six™.

The Simple Six™ answers the two most important business questions: 1) Are we making money? and 2) Are we meeting Customer requirements for quality, volume, time, and cost?

Mission Simple's Simple Six™:

1. **Revenue** – The cash received in a specific duration of time (should not include uncollected billings – time spent collecting payment is waste).

2. **FTE** – Full-time-equivalent is the percent of an employee's full-time hours the employee spends performing specific work (1.0 FTE is generally accepted

---

[6.1]***The Goal**, Eliyahu M. Goldratt and Jeff Cox

Figure 6.1

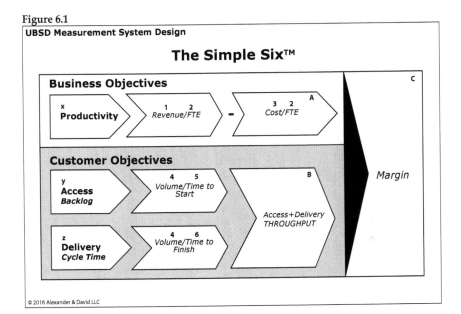

as 2080 hours per year).

3. **Cost** — The total costs for a specific duration time (e.g. month, week, day).

4. **Volume** — The quantity of product or services produced or delivered in a specified duration of time.

5. **Time to Start** — The duration of time from the minute an order is received until the Production System begins work.

6. **Time to Finish** — The duration of time from the minute the Production System begins work until the Customer receives value.

We caution businesses to keep the Simple Six™ simple. Too often, businesses will drill down into the data weeds and get lost trying to make connections between multiple types data. When your efforts are becoming too complex—you're in the weeds. The measures must be uniform and repeatable across the entire system.

IMPACT ON THE CURRENT STATE

The primary impact of the MSD on the current state is the data collection demands the MSD introduces on front line team members. Initially, the front line workers will view the data collection demands as a burden or disruption. However, once the front line team understands the value and purpose of the MSD, they will adopt the additional demands quickly and with fervor.

Another challenge to the current state will be how to reconcile the difference between familiar types of measurement and the MSD. This dynamic is connected to the same challenges confronting the shift from managing the capabilities of people to managing the capabilities of processes.

We tend to measure the wrong things when we attempt to manage wide variation in order to sustain incapable processes. For example, we will invest a great deal of time and resources in "quality review" and "rework" rather than simply fixing the process. It is natural then to want to measure those activities. Unfortunately, we end up measuring waste. This type of data promotes the investment of time and resources on activities that are waste. The data only reinforces the frustration inherent in trying to manage processes with such a wide range of variation. Inevitably, we blame the people doing the work—which only serves to maintain the reliance on the exceptional efforts of the few.

Part 2
Barriers to Exceptional Business Performance

Fallacy - *noun*, a wrong belief, a false or mistaken idea.

—Merriam-Webster

7
The Fallacy of
Exceptional Effort

"When did leaving work on time become an act of courage?"

— 2015 Hyundai Tucson TV ad

SUPERGIRL

"I lost another one," the manager shared and then took a swallow of his micro-brew.

"An order?" I asked.

"No," he replied. "Jane left."

"Jane?"

"Yeah," he sighed. "She'd been my right hand for ten years."

"Do you know why she left?"

He turned and looked at me, "I haven't got a clue. You know, it seems we're losing more and more good people. I am spending way too much time interviewing new employee candidates."

"What did she tell you when she left?" I asked.

"Nothing really," he replied. "I should have seen the signs. She was using up a lot of her PTO—and she hadn't used any PTO in four years."

He grabbed a pretzel and another sip of beer. "A month ago, I think, I came into her office and she was just sitting there."

"Crying?"

"No,—not Jane. She was just sitting there almost meditating. I said: 'Jane? Who died?' She looked at me with the saddest look I had ever seen and said: 'No one.'"

"What was Jane's work day like?" I asked.

He was happy to shift off of that image of Jane. "Well, she was a *worker*. I mean she was an animal. I come in around seven every morning and she was always here before me. And I usually leave around seven and she was still working."

"Productive?"

"The best," he sighed. "You can't replace someone like Jane."

"You think she felt appreciated?"

"Hell yes!" He said emphatically. "At one company meeting, I had the guys in marketing Photoshop her picture so she was Supergirl and I used it in my PowerPoint presentation. The entire company loved it. Every quarter, I gave her the maximum bonus for her position."

He was quiet for a moment. It was clear he was missing Jane.

"Why did she have to work such long days?" I asked.

He smiled with pride, "She was my troubleshooter. Whenever there was a problem, she'd fix it."

"And you have a lot of problems that you needed her to fix?"

"Oh yeah! That's what I mean. I have no idea what I'm going to do without her. I'm afraid it's going to fall on me."

"You're the division manager?" I asked.

"Yeah—," he looked at me.

"And you're going to be solving problems in the Production System?"

"Yeah—," he sighed, "—I know. I need to hire someone fast."

"No!" I said. "You need to fix your processes so you stop having problems."

He sat back, surprised at my outburst.

"Bill,—don't you see?" I continued. "Jane burned out. Your broken system chewed her up and now she's gone. And after seeing this, you tell me you're going to do exactly the same thing yourself? You're fifty-five, Bill. Look ahead at the likely outcomes if you assume Jane's workload."

Bill chuckled, "Ha-ha. Sure. It's only for a short time."

"Until you can find some new innocent, hard-working individual to do it. And then you'll chew them up until they have nothing left and then they'll leave."

He gave me a dark look, "What are you saying? That I'm not pulling my weight?"

"It's not about people," I explained. "It's not about effort. If any single worker is required to deliver exceptional effort in order to execute a process, then the process is ineffective. And typically that means the process variation is really wide."

He sipped his beer and then said, "Explain wide variation."

"Wide variation exists when the results of a process have such a large range of variation that it meets the Customer's requirements less than fifty percent of the time. The rest of the time it requires the exceptional effort of one or more workers in order to meet Customer requirements. You're meeting your Customer's requirements, but the cost is staggering. And the biggest cost is the loss of people like Jane."

Slowly, he nodded. He understood.

"Fixing our processes—," he paused. "That would be a monstrous task. I don't even know where to start."

"It's simple," I explained. "It just looks complex because you're in the weeds. The first thing you have to do is allow your processes to fail."

"What?" He was petrified.

"It's the only way you will truly know which processes are capable of meeting Customer requirements and which are not. You're going to find that more than fifty percent are capable. Otherwise you'd be drowning in losses. Once you've identified the incapable processes, you fix them."

"It's that simple?" he asked.

"Yes," I replied. "It will take longer to find a replacement for Jane then it will to fix your processes. And who knows—if you fix your processes, Jane might actually want to work here again."

Bill looked at me: "You think?"

"Fix the processes first," I said.

"Right."

DESCRIPTION

Mission Simple's Fallacy of Exceptional Effort states that the current, widely-accepted belief that exceptional effort is required to achieve success is actually a fallacy. Further, that exceptional effort is actually waste and works against achieving sustainable success—and rewarding and celebrating exceptional effort perpetuates the waste. If John Wayne were still alive, he'd probably reply: "Them's fightin' words!"

Of all the *stuff* that defines being an American, the belief in exceptional effort has to be right near the top.

The celebrated football coach Vince Lombardi[7.1] led the Green Bay Packers to five National Football League championships in seven years. The Packers, under Lombardi, won the first two Super Bowls. He is enshrined in the Pro Football Hall of Fame and the Super Bowl trophy bears his name. There's no question Lombardi's achievements were exceptional. To achieve these results, Lombardi managed his team based on exceptional effort. In a word, he was relentless.

Jerry Kramer[7.2] played for the Green Bay Packers when Lombardi first came to town. Later, he became an accomplished author and speaker. He describes his first team meeting with Lombardi as a defining moment for himself and his teammates.

Lombardi told his new team: "If you're not willing to make the sacrifice, to pay the price, to put the team first and to subjugate all your individual needs, wishes and wants, then get the hell out."

During that first training camp, a scout from the St. Louis Cardinals who had been watching the Packers practices told Kramer: "Jerry, I've been in this business for 25 years. If the Cardinals had to do this, half of them would quit and the other half would die." Lombardi was relentless. He said: "I firmly believe that any man's finest hour, the greatest fulfillment of all that he holds dear, is that moment when he has worked his heart out in a good cause and lies exhausted on the field of battle—victorious."

[7.1]**Vince Lombardi** was Head Coach of the Green Bay Packers from 1959 to 1967. During his tenure, the Green Bay Packers won five NFL Championships and Super Bowls I and II. His record was 105 wins, 35 losses and 6 ties.

[7.2]**Jerry Kramer** played right guard for the Green Bay Packers from 1958 to 1968. He is author of *Instant Replay, Farewell to Football,* and *Distant Replay* all with Dick Schaap. He also edited *Lombardi: Winning is the Only Thing.*

Lombardi's work ethic was not unique in American culture. In fact, it exemplified it. In short, life in America after World War II was about hard work. "The only place success comes before work is in the dictionary," Lombardi said. "Leaders aren't born they are made. And they are made just like anything else, through hard work. And that's the price we'll have to pay to achieve that goal, or any goal."

In America, the passion to win drives the need for exceptional effort. America's heroes, from the Founding Fathers to *The Right Stuff*[73] of John Glenn and Neil Armstrong, are role models affirming the value of exceptional effort. There are numerous stories of individuals with average capabilities, who, through hard work and commitment, rose to accomplish extraordinary things. As Americans, we are hard-wired from birth to equate exceptional effort with success. We believe we can increase our capabilities through shear will. An emotional Notre Dame football coach Knute Rockne in the locker room said: "Let's win one for the Gipper." An impassioned Theodore Roosevelt stated: "It is only through labor and painful effort, by grim energy and resolute courage, that we move on to better things."

How can this be a fallacy?

IMPACT ON EFFECTIVENESS AND SUSTAINABILITY

It is inevitable that the spirit of exceptional effort would permeate the culture of our organizations. With the weight of history and cultural habits driving organizations to manage the exceptional performance of individuals, how is it possible that this is a fallacy? Was Vince Lombardi wrong?

The answer is yes and no. If you have a process that has a wide range of variation, then the only effective way to achieve consistent results is through exceptional effort. There is no question that sports, and especially team sports, has a wide range of variation.

In only his second season in the NFL, quarterback Dan Marino led the Miami Dolphins to the Super Bowl—and lost. His only consolation was he was young, talented and certainly would have another chance at winning the Super Bowl. In his seventeen-year

[73]*The Right Stuff*, Tom Wolfe

career, Dan Marino and the Dolphins made the playoffs ten times, but Dan never made it back to the Super Bowl again.

The New York Yankees are one of the few teams to stay at the top for any length of time. They achieve this by replacing exceptional players regularly and their payroll consistently ranks the highest in baseball. Since 1998, the Yankees have had either the highest or second highest payroll in Major League Baseball.[7.4] In an eighteen-year span, the New York Yankees won the World Series four times (25%); won the American League Championship Series (ALCS) five times (33%); and made the playoffs fourteen times (78%).

Year	Payroll Rank[7.5]	Result[7.5]
1998	2	**World Series - Won**
1999	1	**World Series - Won**
2000	1	**World Series - Won**
2001	1	ALCS[7.6]
2002	1	ALDS[7.7]
2003	1	World Series - Lost
2004	1	ALDS
2005	1	ALCS
2006	1	ALDS
2007	1	ALDS
2008	1	Missed playoffs
2009	1	**World Series - Won**
2010	1	ALCS
2011	1	ALDS
2012	1	ALCS
2013	1	Missed playoffs
2014	2	Missed playoffs
2015	2	Missed playoffs

If we define exceptional performance in baseball as making the playoffs, the New York Yankees achieve it 78% of the time and fail 22% of the time. In order to achieve success 78% of the time their costs are the highest in their industry. In comparison, the 2015 World Series Champion Kansas City Royals achieved success

[7.4]**MLB Players Association**
[7.5]**Baseball-reference.com**
[7.6]**American League Championship Series**
[7.7]**American League Division Series**

spending 47% less than the Yankees. But their variation was significantly greater. In the same period (1998-2015), the Royals made the playoffs twice, won the ALCS twice, and won the World Series once: Two years at peak, and sixteen years off peak.

Is it possible to manage a process with a wide range of variation to consistently achieve required results? To a limited extent; yes. But the cost is incredibly high and requires exceptional effort as well as considerable luck.

Consider this, Vince Lombardi coached the Packers for nine years, from 1959 to 1967. What was the cost of victory? Of the original 37-man Packer roster in 1959, only nine players were still on the team in 1967 (Bart Starr, Bob Skoronski, Boyd Dowler, Forrest Gregg, Fuzzy Thurston, Henry Jordan, Jerry Kramer, Max McGee, and Ray Nitschke). Less than 25% made it from 1959 to 1967—and only 19% of the 1959 starters were still starters in 1967. How sustainable would a business be if it had to replace 80% of its work force every nine years?

Managing unstable processes creates waste and costs that threaten the sustainability of the organization. It turns front line workers and managers into invisible heroes who manually manipulate processes with wide variation to ensure they meet requirements. The results are not real because exceptional effort is required to make them effective. These processes have a high cost being paid by the workers rather than the business. The toll impacts workers mentally, physically and emotionally making the exceptional effort unsustainable.[7.8]

- *80% of workers feel stress on the job, nearly half say they need help in learning how to manage stress and 42% say their coworkers need such help;*

- *14% of respondents had felt like striking a coworker in the past year, but didn't;*

- *25% have felt like screaming or shouting because of job stress, 10% are concerned about an individual at work they fear could become violent;*

- *9% are aware of an assault or violent act in their workplace*

[7.8] **The American Institute of Stress** study *Attitudes in the American Workplace VII*

and 18% had experienced some sort of threat or verbal
intimidation in the past year

We perpetuate the fallacy of exceptional effort by elevating it with phrases like "work ethic" and we connect the behavior to our heroes and those who have achieved the greatest success — and exceptional effort is no longer considered "exceptional," — it's expected.

A 2015 Hyundai Tucson TV ad exposes our obsession with exceptional effort with its rebellious question: "When did leaving work on time become an act of courage?"

THE REMEDY

The remedy to exceptional effort is to improve or redesign the processes to deliver results with a narrow range of variation. Processes with narrow ranges of variation require no exceptional effort; rather, they simply require standard effort. This significantly reduces costs because the waste of exceptional effort is eliminated. We describe these processes as stable, repeatable and reproducible.

Many professionals (e.g. physicians, engineers, consultants, etc.) will be challenged by efforts to reduce exceptional effort because their value — their education, experience and expertise — is defined by their ability to manage processes with wide variation. In fact, they view narrow variation as mundane and of low value.

If we define value as the ability to handle wide variation, then they are correct. However, in a business system, value is not defined locally — at a single individual or function level — it is defined at a system level. At a system level, throughput speed defines value, not individual contribution. Whatever improves throughput speed adds value and whatever slows throughput speed adds waste. Wide variation slows throughput speed. Therefore, we must reduce variation in order to improve throughput speed.

If the objective is to reduce variation, then investing in resources capable of managing variation is waste. We must understand that the resources are not waste; the variation is waste. The resources are the cost of the waste created by the variation.

8
The Fallacy of Exceeding Expectations

"Good enough is great."

— Marcus A. Oksa, MS, RCP

EVERYONE HAS TO WORK A LITTLE HARDER IN TODAY'S MARKET

"We can't just meet their expectations—we have to exceed them!" the President said, slamming his fist on the conference room table.

The group was quiet.

"For what purpose," I asked. The President turned toward me.

"Look," he said. "Our markets have gotten more and more competitive. There are more players and it's harder to win business and keep business. Exceeding expectations is what we have to do to compete."

"Is your customer churn rate higher today than it was five years ago?" I pressed.

He thought for a moment and turned to his VP of Sales, "George?"

The VP of Sales quickly thumbed through a report and replied, "Well—yes—it is higher."

The President gave me a victorious grin. "See!"

"Why?"

"More competition!" he cried.

"Are you delivering the most quality, in the shortest time, at the lowest cost?"

He paused for a moment. He looked around the room. His eyes focused on his VP of Operations.

The VP of Operations offered: "We've been having some problems with customer complaints. They're complaining about quality and on-time delivery. It's creating rework."

"And you're losing customers because of this?" I asked.

The VP of Sales interrupted: "Yes. A number of customers have told us our quality and on-time delivery is just not meeting their requirements."

The President said: "You understand now. We have to begin exceeding our customers' expectations or we're going to lose our position in the market."

"Actually, —I think you need to begin *meeting* your customers' expectations first," I said.

The VP of Operations nodded. "Good point."

"We have to do better than that!" the President exclaimed.

"Why?" I asked.

"We're losing customers!" He argued.

"That's because you're not *meeting* requirements. It's not because you're not *exceeding* them."

"Well—our competitors are meeting requirements,—so we must be better in order to win the business back," the President said.

I turned to the VP of Operations, "You have control charts?"

He nodded.

"Does the *mean* of your process capabilities exceed the customers' requirements?" I asked.

He nodded.

"What's the range of variation?"

"Not so good," he sighed.

"What's the percentage of time you meet or exceed customer requirements?" I asked.

"About seventy percent," he said.

"And five years ago?"

"Better than ninety-five percent," he said with pride.

"What changed?"

The VP of Operations hesitated and looked at the VP of Sales. The President was confused. He truly wasn't following the conversation.

The VP of Sales broke the silence: "Two years ago we wanted to expand our market and go after ABC Inc., a customer of our biggest competitor. Remember, Ed?" He was looking at the President.

The President nodded. "Okay — what's that have to do with this?"

"ABC Inc. told us if we wanted to win the business we had to beat our competitor's delivery times," the VP of Sales explained.

"Right," the President said. "I remember."

"And you said, 'We can do it,' and they said we had the business," the VP of Sales was looking at his hands.

The VP of Operations turned to the President, "You never told me about this."

Suddenly defensive, the President replied: "Look — everyone has to work a little harder in today's market."

"We don't have the capabilities to meet their requirements," the VP of Operations said flatly. "The only way we've been able to do it is at the expense of other customers. And they're getting pissed and leaving."

The President slowly sat down in his chair and frowned.

I said: "So the noble desire to win a major customer away from a competitor has resulted in an increase in customer churn."

The President looked at me and said, "I guess so."

I continued: "And the remedy is to double down and do it again?"

The President sighed, "What's the alternative?"

"Redesign your processes to meet your customers' true

requirements and blow the competition out of the water," I said.

"Is that possible?" he asked.

The VP of Operations nodded.

I continued: "But let's be sure the value we deliver aligns with what our customer is willing to pay for, or it's waste and we'll be right back in the same boat."

The President smiled and said: "I'd love to blow my competition out of the water."

DESCRIPTION

The widespread reliance on *exceptional effort* is not the result of management or the front line team. It is deeply entrenched in the culture of the organization. Management invests in resources to manage variation rather than reducing variation. Front line workers seek to improve their status in the organization by demonstrating exceptional effort in managing the variation. The dysfunction of exceptional effort is further compounded by The Fallacy of Exceeding Expectations.

The Fallacy of Exceeding Expectations states that the current, widely-accepted belief that exceeding expectations increases value to the Customer is actually a fallacy — and the investment in exceeding expectations is also waste and works against achieving sustainable success.

There are ad men and salesmen rolling over in their martini's right now. Sorry gents, but it's true.

The dysfunction of exceeding expectations also promotes exceptional effort. Unlike the exceptional effort required to manage wide variation, the exceptional effort required to support exceeding expectations artificially raises the requirements beyond what the Customer is willing to pay for and therefore what the organization is willing to pay for. Who pays for it? The front line worker — and the Customer in the form of increased failure rates.

IMPACT ON EFFECTIVENESS AND SUSTAINABILITY

Increased competition drives the need for businesses to reach ever higher for differentiation. One of the most common tactics is to deliver more than what the Customer is asking for or is willing to pay for. In a competitive environment, this tactic flourishes under the assumption that Customers value it.

Dave Thomas, founder of the Wendy's fast food restaurant chain, made the following promise to his Customers: "Our goal must be to exceed our customers' expectations every day." Dave was only following the lead set by many other organizations seeking competitive advantage. He was also lured by the fallacy that exceeding expectations increases value.

When businesses seek competitive differentiation by exceeding Customer expectations, their costs go up, but their revenue does not. Why? Promoting the philsophy of exceeding expectations turns everyone in the organization into a problem-solver. When the front line team is solving problems, they are not executing processes — throughput slows down, costs and failure rates go up. Efforts to exceed Customer expectations increase the cost to win the same business at the same price. In order to win business, Sales increases promises to the Customer beyond the Work System's capabilities and then badgers the Work System to provide exceptional effort to meet them. This type of dysfunction can cascade and quickly destroy a business when costs out-pace revenue and failure rates drive Customers away.

What begins as an innocent, noble tactic of delivering more service to the Customer becomes one of the most threatening challenges to sustainability. This noble but misguided approach is destroying business through runaway cost and disrupted throughput.

It is likely we have all worked in an organization that behaves like this. Many of us work in one now. As with so many fallacies, the fundamental driver behind its continued use is the compelling power of its noble premise: "Exceed our customers' expectations every day." How can that goal be bad? The tragedy is the cost of simply redesigning the process to meet the new requirements is but a grain of sand when compared with the overwhelming sea of destructive cost created by the exceptional effort to make incapable processes achieve higher requirements.

As prevalent as the fallacy of exceeding expectations is throughout our business culture, one would think that exceeding expectations must deliver distinctive value to the Customer relationship—the ROI must be considerable. In truth, it's just the opposite. The investment in exceeding expectations has a negative ROI.

According to Mike Wooden, Chief Commercial Officer for Convergys, "Exceeding expectations typically requires significant investments in time, money, and implementation that have either a very short-term ROI impact or one that evaporates almost the minute you have deployed it."

Wooden calls this effect "satisficing." He says, "continued investments in trying to strive for exceeding expectations simply raises the bar to meet expectations, costs a lot of money and ultimately doesn't make anyone more loyal."[8.1]

How can this be? The fundamental truth is Customers want their expectations met and they are willing to pay to have them met but they place little or no value in getting more than expected —or more than what they are willing to pay for. What Customers really value is trust that their expectations will be met. We call this: "good enough is great."

With everyone striving to exceed expectations, why is it that Customers are primarily concerned with simply meeting expectations? It's because their expectations are met less than 66% of the time.[8.1] It is clear that businesses would be better served improving their effectiveness in *adequately meeting* expectations rather than investing in trying to *exceed* them.

REMEDY

Exceeding expectations increases the exceptional effort required to artificially raise the requirements beyond what the Customer is willing to pay for and therefore what the organization is willing to pay for. When businesses seek competitive differentiation by exceeding Customer expectations, their costs go up, but their prices do not.

The remedy is to stop trying to exceed expectations. Exceeding

[8.1]**Wooden, Mike**, "It Doesn't Pay to Exceed Expectations for Customer Service," TCMnet. com, April 17, 2015

expectations does not add value to the Customer and therefore any cost in resources or dollars is waste. If the Customer places real value —value they're willing to pay for—in better performance results, then R&D should be tasked to redesign the current processes or design new processes.

9
The Fallacy of Managing by Accountability

"You can hold people accountable to follow a process — but you cannot hold people accountable for the results of a process they have followed."

—Marcus A. Oksa, MS, RCP

THEY'RE NOT HORSES, THEY'RE PEOPLE

"Whatever happened to professional sales people?" my friend asked as he carefully sipped his single malt. He gave me a studied look and demanded: "Tell me — where are they?"

He was a young 60, Vice President of Sales, and a lifelong friend.

"Are your sales down, Jack?" I asked.

"Ugh," he groaned. "They've been down for five years. In five years, I haven't once hit my numbers."

"What's the problem?"

"I've got one —," he paused, " — maybe two good sales people."

He shifted in his bar stool, grabbed a shrimp and waved it at me: "I've tried everything. Bonuses, commissions, vacations, cars.

Nothing works. I'm telling you. I just don't know what motivates these people anymore."

"Are they following your sales processes?"

"Huh?" he raised his eyebrows. "They're sales people. They know our product. They know our pricing. They know how to negotiate. What the hell else is there?"

"What are your sales processes?" I probed further.

"I don't understand," he blinked and took another sip of his scotch.

"You must have processes your sales people follow," I explained.

"They have a territory and they're supposed to go out and get the business. They know how to sell. Well — some of them do."

"Jack, a process is a sequence of linked activities that when performed produce a predictable result," I said.

"Aww — geez," he said. "I'm not an engineer, I'm a salesman."

"Right — but you have a routine you follow. True?"

He looked at me cautiously: "Yeah."

"Does everyone follow your routine?"

"Not really," he said. "Everyone's got their own way of doing it. It's a style thing."

"Exactly. That's your problem."

"Huh?"

I paused to sip my beer and then said: "Jack — are you a good salesman?"

"One of the best," he smiled.

"Then your routine is effective."

"I guess."

"If another sales person followed your routine would they get the same results?"

His eyes twinkled and a sly grin rose on his face, "Not as good as me."

"Okay. You're special," I smiled. "But the routine is what makes you special — right?"

"Maybe," he conceded.

"It's your secret recipe."

"Yes!" he exclaimed. "That is absolutely true."

"What would happen if all of your sales team followed your

routine?"

He thought for moment: "Followed it exactly?"

"Yes," I said. "Exactly."

"I see what you're getting at," he said. "But they won't do that. They are all fighting for commission and they're independent thinkers. They all think they're experts. They're not going to listen to an old timer like me."

"They will listen — if you eliminate the commissions and all of the other incentives."

He burst into a big belly laugh that went on for a moment until tears welled up in his eyes.

"You're a funny man," he sighed, wiping the tears away.

"Your problem is not performance, commitment or competence. It's variation," I explained.

He continued to wipe his eyes but he was listening.

"Every member of your sales team is using a different process and your results show it. The effectiveness of your team is all over the place — from good to terrible. You immediately think your problem is a *people* issue, and you've got to manage the people — so you go to carrots and sticks. They're not horses, they're people."

"What else can I do," he asked.

"Document your routine as a process. Train your team in your process. Then measure the results of the process over time. This will tell you the capabilities and variation of your process. If the variation is reasonably narrow and the capabilities meet your requirements, then eliminate the commissions, raise their salaries and pay them as professionals, not as performers."

"And if the process capabilities don't meet my requirements?" he asked.

"Then redesign them, test the new designs and adjust."

He thought for a moment, "It might work. But it seems like a big risk."

"When was the last time you hit your numbers?" I asked.

"Good point."

DESCRIPTION

The Fallacy of Managing by Accountability states that the current, widely-accepted belief that leaders and managers can achieve required results by holding workers accountable for the results of processes they have followed is a fallacy. This fallacy also fuels the fallacies of exceptional effort and exceeding expectations.

The Fallacy of Managing by Accountability is built on the belief that the value of a worker is defined by the worker's ability to manage the results of processes with wide variation. Rather than managing the processes, we use carrots and sticks to manage the people — through exceptional effort — to artificially force unstable processes to produce required results. This is waste compounded exponentially. Any leader who employs carrots and sticks as a viable method of achieving process results is failing — and their business system is ineffective and unsustainable.

IMPACT ON EFFECTIVENESS AND SUSTAINABILITY

If our assessment of the negative impact of managing by accountability appears severe, it is due to the severe negative impact it has on the organization. In order to visualize the impact, let's review what promotes effectiveness and sustainability.

Organizations achieve effectiveness and sustainability through *exceptional business performance* defined as delivering the most value, in the shortest time, at the lowest cost with processes that are stable, repeatable and reproducible. We measure business performance with throughput, inventory and operating costs. The simple way to understand this is to focus on *throughput*. Anything that increases the speed of throughput is good, anything that slows throughput is bad.

Fast throughput = low cost, high margin

Slow throughput = high cost, low margin

Slow throughput makes a business system ineffective and unsustainable. Managing by accountability does not improve throughput speed. Rather, it focuses on managing the waste verses fixing the cause. It turns everyone into a problem-solver. Problem-solving in the Work System slows throughput, increases cost and increases failure to meet requirements.

Managing by accountability assumes that there is a correlation between the front line workers' "effectiveness" to manage variation and throughput speed. In truth, the relationship is inverse. Investing in managing and sustaining the dysfunction of wide variation reduces throughput speed and increases costs. Narrow variation delivers increased throughput speed with no exceptional effort and wide variation delivers slow throughput speed and requires significant exceptional effort. The primary barrier to throughput speed is a process with wide variation. Let's review an example.

At ABC Consulting, proposals are required to win engagements with new Customers. The proposals are critical to ABC's success. ABC has a specialist who drafts proposals and that specialist is very skilled at creating proposals that win business. ABC pays the specialist a hefty salary and a bonus based on the volume of business their proposals win. At ABC, all proposals go through the specialist—no one else can do a proposal. This situation leads to many long nights, lost weekends and few vacations—and when the specialist is sick, no proposals are produced and work backs up.

Our example describes a process with wide variation: creating a proposal. We know this because ABC has no confidence in the results of the process and therefore places all of their confidence in the capabilities of a person. ABC compounds this barrier to throughput, by paying a high salary and bonus (carrot) to manage

Figure 9.1

ABC Consulting Proposal Process	Current State	Future State
Cost of Worker to Execute the Process	$125,000	$35,000
Carrots (Bonus)	$50,000	$0
Total Cost	$175,000	$35,000
WASTE >>	**$140,000**	

the ineffective process; and the specialist is achieving results through exceptional effort. Finally, if the specialist produces a proposal that fails to win business, ABC holds the specialist accountable.

How much waste do you see? (Figure 9.1) What would happen to ABC's bottom line if the process of producing proposals had narrow variation? The specialist would not be required to manage the wide variation or waste. That specialist could perform work that adds value to ABC's Customers, increasing revenue without adding cost.

We're not suggesting ABC's proposals are not needed or that they are any less critical to ABC's success. However, proposals are what we call NVR's (non-value-added but required). The Customer does not pay ABC consulting to produce a proposal, therefore producing a proposal does not deliver value to the Customer. But ABC cannot receive revenue without a proposal. NVR's are waste—no matter their importance. ABC's highest priority should be to reduce the waste created by NVR's to the lowest possible level. However, our example illustrates that ABC is doing just the opposite.

The problem is not the effectiveness of the individual— managing by accountability—the problem is the wide variation. When the remedy is managing by accountability; the organization is compounding waste.

Consider this...

One day, at a paper mill in Wisconsin, workers noticed water on the floor in the plant. They looked around and couldn't find the source. Their remedy? They dragged a barrel over and positioned it to catch the water.

By mid-day the barrel was full. It took four men to drag the barrel full of water outside and dump it. This activity continued for a week. Six times every twenty-four hours. The managers realized changing the barrels was costing them lost work time so they called engineering and requested a solution.

Engineering examined the situation and concluded they needed a way to catch the water and automatically remove it. They constructed a catch basin, added a large pump and built a pipeline to an external wall. They created a hole in the wall for the pipe to exit the building and a gravel spill area to dissipate the water.

No one thought of fixing the leak.

REMEDY

Managing by accountability is a waste-compounding remedy employed by managers to induce exceptional effort from front line workers to overcome the dysfunction of processes with wide variation. It places responsibility on workers to deliver exceptional effort to force an ineffective process to meet requirements. The remedy is to fix the process. When a process has narrow variation it is stable and capable of being repeatable and reproducible. Repeatable means the range of variation is consistent when the process is performed by the same individual over time. Reproducible means the range of variation is consistent when the process is performed by different individuals over time (Figure 9.2).

The remedy? Focus on fixing the leak, not how effectively workers manage the leak.

Figure 9.2

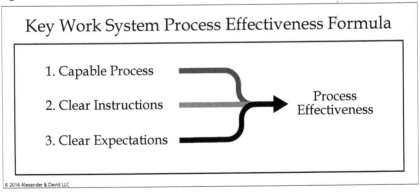

Key Work System Process Effectiveness Formula

1. Capable Process

2. Clear Instructions

Process Effectiveness

3. Clear Expectations

© 2016 Alexander & David LLC

Parts 1 & 2
Summary & Review

Before we dive into the architecture of Customer-Supplier Relationships and the UBSD, let's take a moment to review.

At this point, we have presented the principles of Mission Simple and the five key parts of Customer-Supplier Relationships and the UBSD:

1. *Customer-Supplier Relationships*
2. *The Universal Business System Design*
3. *Managing Process Capabilities*
4. *Quantitative Alignment*
5. *Measurement System Design*

We have also presented the three common fallacies that prevent organizations from achieving exceptional business performance.

1. *The Fallacy of Exceptional Effort*
2. *The Fallacy of Exceeding Expectations*

3. *The Fallacy of Managing by Accountability*

Before we move to the system design and process flow details of the UBSD, it is important that you are comfortable with your understanding of the five key elements and the fallacies.

Spend a few moments working through the list below. This is the knowledge base of the UBSD and Customer-Supplier Relationships. If you dive into the next 19 chapters before you are comfortable with your understanding of the information below, your journey may be confusing and overwhelming.

PART 1 - KEY POINTS

1. ***Mission Simple*** — Mission Simple provides organizations with a highly effective methodology for achieving Performance Excellence through exceptional business performance. It consists of three principles:

    a. *Customer-Supplier Relationships*

    b. *Decision-Maker/Problem-Solver*

    c. *Culture & Risk*

2. ***Customer-Supplier Relationships*** — define the quantitative rules governing the relationships between Customers and Suppliers both internally and externally.

3. ***The Universal Business System Design (UBSD)*** — provides a universal framework to support Customer-Supplier Relationships. It consists of three core parts:

    a. *Key Work Systems or KWS's*

    b. *Key Work Processes or KWP's*

    c. *Key UBSD Processes or KUP's*

4. ***Managing Process Capabilities*** — shifts the method of achieving business performance results from managing the capabilities of people (wide variation) to managing the capabilities of processes (narrow variation).

5. ***Quantitative Alignment*** — aligns the organization's four core constituents quantitatively: Executive Stakeholders, Customers, Suppliers and the Work System. Quantitative Alignment eliminates wide variation and the associated waste — and provides objective evidence that the Work System is investing time and resources *only* on efforts that impact the Executive Stakeholders' and Customers' quantitative objectives.

6. ***Measurement System Design*** — provides the critical quantitative data needed to manage the capabilities of processes.

PART 2 - KEY POINTS

1. ***The Fallacy of Exceptional Effort*** — states that the current, widely-accepted belief that exceptional effort is required to achieve success is actually a fallacy. Exceptional effort is actually waste as it's primary application is to manage unstable, incapable processes with wide variation.

2. ***The Fallacy of Exceeding Expectations*** — states that the current, widely-accepted belief that exceeding expectations increases value to the Customer is actually a fallacy — and the investment in exceeding expectations is also waste.

3. ***The Fallacy of Managing by Accountability*** — states that the current, widely-accepted belief that leaders and managers can achieve required results by holding workers accountable is a fallacy — is built on the false belief that the value of a worker is defined by the worker's ability to manage unstable, incapable processes with wide variation — and, rather than fix the processes, the workers can be induced to deliver exceptional effort to maintain dysfunctional processes through the use carrots and sticks.

THE MISSION SIMPLE GLOSSARY

1. ***Exceptional business performance*** — describes the state in which an organization is both effective and sustainable, delivering the *most value*, in the *shortest time*, for the *lowest cost*.

2. ***Sustainable improvement*** — requires quantitative measurement and quantitative alignment.

3. ***Effective*** — describes a system or process that delivers the *most value*, in the *shortest time*, for the *lowest cost*.

4. ***Sustainable*** — describes a system or process that is stable, repeatable and reproducible.

5. ***Wide Variation*** — is the primary cause of waste and cost in an organization.

6. ***The Simple Six™*** — are the universal measures supporting the Measurement System Design or MSD. They consist of the following:

   i.   *Revenue*

   ii. *FTE*

   iii. *Cost*

   iv. *Volume*

   v.   *Time-to-Start*

   vi. *Time-to-Finish*

7. ***Local Optimization*** — occurs when individual Key Work Systems solve their own problems independent of the business system. This is the most common method problems are resolved in most organizations but it is also the primary creator of system waste. ***Business System Optimization*** is a more effective method of resolving problems because it reduces waste rather than creating waste.

8. ***Throughput*** — is the rate the business system generates cash through sales. We also refer to throughput as the "speed to value."

9. ***Key Work Systems (KWS's)*** — are fundamental parts of the UBSD. A KWS contains one or more processes that transform inputs into higher value outputs. There are seven KWS in the UBSD:

     i.   Leadership

     ii.   Sales

     iii.   CSQA

     iv.   Research & Development (R&D)

     v.   Business System Control (BSC)

     vi.   Supplier

     vii.   Production System

10. ***Key Work Processes (KWP's)*** — are "intra" processes and reside solely "within" a single KWS. Collectively, the KWP's produce the output of the KWS.

11. ***Key UBSD Processes (KUP's)*** — are "inter" processes and reside "between" multiple KWS, linking them to produce specific deliverables or value to the Customer.

SUMMARY

We have distilled the first nine chapters into the list above to help you focus on the critical learnings required to understand the value and impact of Customer-Supplier Relationships and the UBSD. Despite our best efforts to simplify this knowledge base, it's scope can still be daunting.

Here is a simple way to capture the essence of the knowledge base:

Play your position.

Have you ever watched junior or mite hockey? Soccer? What you notice among children under the age of 10 who are just learning the game is they struggle with *playing position*. Wherever the ball goes or puck goes, there is a little crowd of children following it. This is what most organizations look like. Rather than functioning as a high performing team with everyone playing their positions in a disciplined way, it is every person for themselves.

Why is this case? Two reasons:

1. *The current processes are unstable with wide variation and as such are incapable of meeting Customer requirements without the exceptional effort of the front line workers. Rather than investing in redesigning processes, organizations simply invest in staff to correct failure at the point failure becomes visible.*

2. *There is a chronic absence of adequate supply to every Key Work System. In order to get the job done, its every person for themselves as they chase through the organization to secure supply. They* game *the system and create internal gray markets adding unimaginable cost to the operation.*

Mission Simple helps the organization shift its unstable processes with wide variation to stable processes with narrow variation — and it ensures there is always adequate supply to every Key Work System so that each player can remain discplined to playing their position.

If you can keep this simple message in mind as you explore the next 19 chapters on the system design and work flow of the UBSD, you will discover an incredible world of opportunity to dramatically increase value to your Customers and Executive Stakeholders, and reduce the devastating stress in your current Work System.

Part 3
Key Work Systems of the UBSD

Figure P3.1

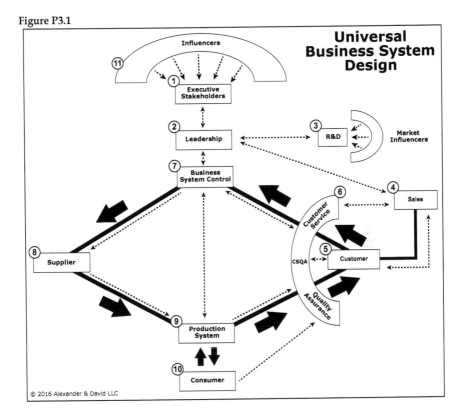

INTRODUCTION TO KEY WORK SYSTEMS

In the next seven chapters, we provide in-depth descriptions of each Key Work System shown in Figure P3.1. Key Work Systems (KWS's) are one of the three core parts of the UBSD and contain processes that transform inputs into higher value outputs. There are seven KWS's in the UBSD:

1. *Leadership*
2. *Sales*
3. *CSQA*
4. *Research & Development (R&D)*
5. *Business System Control (BSC)*
6. *Supplier*

7. Production System

WHY IS THIS IMPORTANT

If you are familiar with team sports, you understand that there are positions that each player occupies. When you look at the UBSD, think of the KWS's as players occupying positions on the field. The next seven chapters describe the positions, their roles and responsibilities, and the processes they execute within their systems.

As we discussed in *Parts 1 & 2 Summary & Review*, most organizations struggle to function as a high performing team because the players are not playing their positions in a disciplined way — too often it is every person for themselves.

The KWS's provide discipline for each key role in the UBSD.

HOW TO READ THE CHAPTERS

Each chapter follows the structure below.

1. ***Description*** — The description section of each chapter describes the primary value contributed by each individual KWS. The *value* is described as transforming inputs into higher value outputs.

2. ***Roles & Responsibilities*** — The roles and responsibilities section describes the role each KWS plays in delivering value to the Customer and the Executive Stakeholders; and the responsibilities of the role in delivering value.

3. ***Key Work Processes*** — The Key Work Process section examines each individual Key Work Process (KWP) within each KWS. Each KWP contributes to the value of the KWS by transforming inputs into higher value outputs. In this section, the key parts of each KWP are defined:

   - **Supplier** - Upstream supplier of inputs
   - **Inputs** - The input being supplied
   - **Process** - The transformation of input into higher value output

- **Outputs** - The higher value output
- **Customer** - The downstream customer

4. ***Key Work Process Diagram***—In addition to the narrative text, each chapter contains a diagram illustrating the suppliers, inputs, processes, outputs and customers for all the KWP's.

HOW TO USE THE KWS'S

Each KWS chapter is designed as a complete, self-contained role description. Once you have identified your KWS's and the corresponding team members, you can use each chapter for education and training purposes.

These chapters also serve as a powerful troubleshooting resource. Once you have a command of the Key Work Systems, you will begin to rapidly identify the causes behind many of the problems you face everyday in your operation—and the remedies offered by following the rules of the KWS's and the UBSD.

THE KWS GLOSSARY

Business Processes — A *business process* is a Key Work Process within a Key Work System that produces outputs of value to the Executive Stakeholders and meets the requirements of Leadership.

Capable Processes — A *capable process* describes a stable process whose capabilities are capable of meeting Customer or Executive Stakeholder requirements.

Communication & Conflict Resolution Plan (CCRP) — A *Communication and Conflict Resolution Plan (CCRP)* defines how CSQA will proactively respond to a Production System process that is not meeting requirements (a problem) and communicates the gap to the Customer while seeking a course of action to meet requirements.

Customer Processes — A *Customer process* is a Key Work Process within a Key Work System that produces outputs of value to the Customer and may or may not meet the requirements of the Customer.

Market Processes — A *market process* is the same as a *Customer process* except that it applies to the objectives of the overall market.

Service Recovery - *Service Recovery* is a Key UBSD Process (KUP) employed when the Work System processes cannot meet Customer requirements. It provides the Customer with one or more external alternatives capable of meeting requirements in order to maintain a relationship in good standing with the Customer.

Work System Processes — A *Work System process* refers to any Key Work Process within the Work System that produces outputs of value to the Executive Stakeholders or the Customer.

10
Leadership

DESCRIPTION

The Leadership Key Work System (KWS) transforms the Executive Stakeholder's *business objectives* into *business requirements*. Leadership delivers the business requirements to three downstream KWS's: Sales, Research & Development (R&D) and Business System Control (BSC).

Leadership also makes *decisions to build or pass* on proposals from R&D. Leadership monitors the process performance of Sales, R&D and the Work System via the data from the Measurement System Design (MSD) to ensure the processes are meeting business requirements.

ROLE & RESPONSIBILITIES

Role:

The role of Leadership is the Executive Stakeholder's gateway to the Work System. Leadership protects the Work System

Figure 10.1

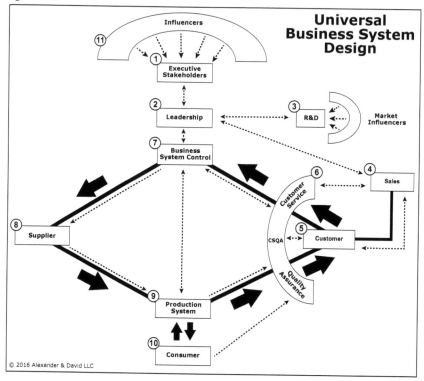

from the waste created when the Executive Stakeholder enters the Work System.

Leadership achieves this through Quantitative Alignment to the Executive Stakeholder's business objectives. Quantitative Alignment confirms that Sales, R&D and the Work System business processes produce results, within established control limits, capable of meeting the business requirements. The only way to give the Executive Stakeholders the confidence necessary to keep them from entering the Work System and creating waste is with quantitative process capabilities aligned to meet Executive Stakeholders objectives.

When the Executive Stakeholder tells the Work System "how" to do what it does, the Work System loses money. When the Work System chooses "how" to meet the

*Executive Stakeholder's requirements, the Work System
makes money.*

In the same way, Leadership must also stay out of the
Work System. This will be challenging to many current state
leaders, who will find they are deeply immersed in the Work
System — and, worse, in the actual Production System. The
litmus test for leaders is this: Leaders do not perform tasks,
they assign tasks to resources, establish requirements and
measure results. When leaders apply this test to their current
state, they typically find a large portion of their time is spent
performing tasks rather than assigning tasks to resources — or
they find they are micro-managing the work being done by
the resources as evidenced by high volumes of phone calls and
emails back and forth with the resources as they perform the
task. This behavior is managing waste.

*Leadership must not perform tasks. When Leadership
performs tasks it is not only waste, but it compounds
waste throughout the business system.*

Leadership is responsible for delivering adequate supply
to three internal customers: BSC, Sales and R&D. In order to
meet this responsibility, Leadership depends on adequate
delivery of supply from its single internal supplier: the
Executive Stakeholders.

Responsibilities:

- Following the Executive Stakeholders' strategic planning
  process, the Executive Stakeholders deliver to Leadership
  the business objectives defined quantitatively as Key
  Performance Indicators (KPI's). Leadership then
  transforms the KPI's into business requirements and
  delivers them to Sales, R&D and Work System.

- R&D regularly produces proposals to implement new
  processes and redesigns of current processes. R&D delivers
  these proposals to Leadership for decisions to approve or
  decline. Leadership has the option to approve or decline

the proposal, or decline it due to inadequate information. The second option allows the proposal to stay alive until adequate information is provided.

LEADERSHIP KEY WORK PROCESSES (KWP's)

Leadership is responsible for five Key Work Processes (KWP's).

1. **02010A**
Transform Sales Business Objectives into Sales Business Requirements
Leadership transforms the *Sales business objectives* into *Sales business requirements.*

Supplier: Executive Stakeholders

Inputs: Sales business objectives

Process: Transform Sales business objectives into Sales business requirements

Outputs: Sales business requirements

Customer: Sales

2. **02020B**
Transform R&D Business Objectives into R&D Business Requirements
Leadership transforms *R&D business objectives* into *R&D business requirements.*

Supplier: Executive Stakeholders

Inputs: R&D business objectives

Process: Transform R&D business objectives into R&D business requirements

Outputs: R&D business requirements

Customer: R&D

3. **02030C**
Transform Work System Business Objectives into Work System Business Requirements
Leadership transforms *Work System business objectives*

Figure 10.2

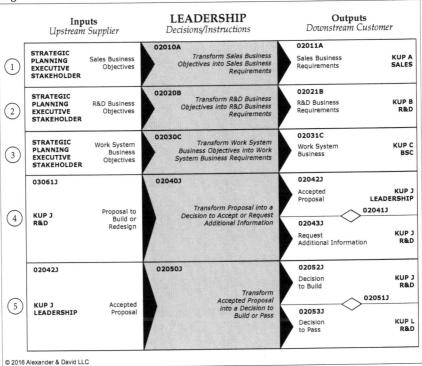

into *Work System business requirements.*

Supplier: Executive Stakeholders

Inputs: Work System business objectives

Process: Transform Work System business objectives into Work System business requirements

Outputs: Work System business requirements

Customer: BSC

4. **02040J**
Transform Proposal into a Decision to Accept or Request Additional Information
   Leadership transforms *proposals to build or redesign* into a *decision* to accept or request additional information.

Supplier: R&D

Inputs: Proposals to build or redesign

Process: Transform proposal to build or redesign into a decision to accept or request additional information

Outputs: Accepted proposal or request for additional information

Customer: Leadership and R&D

5. **02050J**
   Transform Accepted Proposal into a Decision to Build or Pass

   Leadership transforms an *accepted proposal* into a *decision.*

   Supplier: Leadership

   Inputs: Accepted proposal

   Process: Transform accepted proposals into a decision to build or pass

   Outputs: Decision to build or decision to pass

   Customer: R&D

11
Sales

DESCRIPTION

The Sales Key Work System transforms *Sales business requirements* into *new Customer prospects* delivered to CSQA.

ROLE & RESPONSIBILITIES

Role:

The role of Sales is limited to delivering new Customer prospects to CSQA.

Unlike traditional Sales functions, in the UBSD, Sales is responsible solely for delivering Customer prospects to the Work System via CSQA and for documenting the Customer's quantitative objectives. Sales is *not responsible* for managing accounts, writing proposals, or providing customer service. Sales functions as a true "hunter" solely contacting and securing proposal contract opportunities.

Figure 11.1

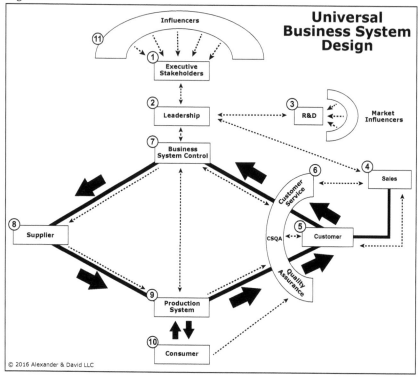

Sales is responsible for delivering adequate supply to two internal UBSD customers: R&D and CSQA; and the external Customer. In order to meet these responsibilities, Sales depends on adequate delivery of supply from three internal suppliers: Leadership, R&D, and CSQA; and the external Customer. The external Customer is both a supplier and a Customer to the UBSD.

Responsibilities:

- Sales receives business requirements from Leadership and aligns them with current Sales business process capabilities to identify the Sales processes capable of meeting the business requirements. If one or more current Sales business processes are determined to be incapable of meeting the business requirements, they are sent to R&D for remedy.

- Once capable processes have been identified, Sales transforms the business requirements into business specifications and delivers them to Sales.

- Sales transforms business specifications into a Customer target list. This list consists of prospects — any Customer not currently engaged with the organization.

- Sales conducts outbound calling to the Customer list to schedule sales appointments. Whenever possible, these appointments should be conducted face-to-face. Since 60% of communication is non-verbal,[11.1] detecting non-verbal cues is critical to the diagnostic process of effective Sales.

- During the sales appointments, Sales employs a diagnostic approach verses a presentation approach. The objective is to identify and confirm the Key Performance Indicators (KPI's) the Customer hopes to improve as a result of an investment in the organization, and the quantitative dollar value of the improvement — and deliver them to CSQA.

- Sales also nurtures *lost Customers*, those Customers for whom the Work System process capabilities and, through the processes of CCRP and Service Recovery, their contracts were lost but the relationships were retained in good standing. Sales nurtures these lost Customers through phone and face-to-face contact until identifying a new opportunity to deliver value and securing a new request for proposal.

SALES KEY WORK PROCESSES (KWP's)

Sales is responsible for six Key Work Processes (KWP's).

1. *04010A*
Transform Sales Business Requirements and Current Sales Business Processes into a Decision Identifying Capable Processes

Sales transforms *Sales business requirements* and *current Sales business processes* into a *decision* that identifies capable processes.

[11.1]**Mehrabian & Wiener**, 1967 and Mehrabian & Ferris, 1967.

Supplier: Leadership and Sales Process Library

Inputs: Sales business requirements and current Sales business processes

Process: Transform Sales business requirements and current Sales business processes into a decision identifying capable processes

Outputs: Capable Sales business processes and requirements or incapable Sales business processes and requirements

Customer: Sales or R&D

2. **04020A**
   Transform Capable Sales Business Processes & Requirements into Sales Business Specifications

   Sales transforms capable *Sales business processes* and *requirements* into *Sales business specifications*.

   Supplier: Sales

   Inputs: Capable Sales business processes and requirements

   Process: Transform capable Sales business processes and requirements into Sales business specifications

   Outputs: Sales business specifications

   Customer: Sales

3. **04030D**
   Transform Sales Business Specifications into Customer Target List

   Sales transforms *Sales business specifications* into a *Customer target list*.

   Supplier: Sales

   Inputs: Sales business specifications

   Process: Transform Sales business specifications into Customer target list

   Outputs: Customer target list

   Customer: Sales

Figure 11.2

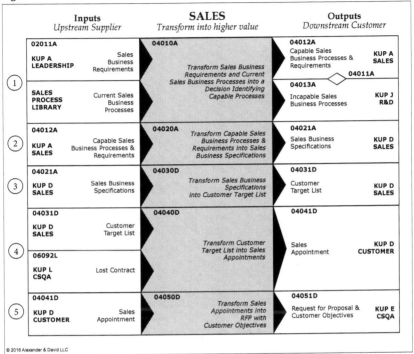

© 2016 Alexander & David LLC

4. 04040D
Transform Customer Target List or Lost Contract into Sales Appointments

Sales transforms the *Customer target list* or *lost contract* into *sales appointments* with prospective Customers.

Supplier: Sales

Inputs: Customer target list and lost contracts

Process: Transform Customer target list or lost contract into sales appointments

Outputs: Sales appointments

Customer: Customer

5. *04050D*

   Transform Sales Appointments into Request for Proposal with Customer Objectives

   Sales transforms *sales appointments* into a *request for proposal* with *Customer quantitative objectives*.

   Supplier: Customer

   Inputs: Sales appointments

   Process: Transform sales appointments into request for proposal and Customer objectives

   Outputs: Request for proposal and Customer objectives

   Customer: CSQA

12
CSQA

DESCRIPTION

The CSQA Key Work System performs both the Customer Service role and the Quality Assurance role.

Unlike traditional Customer Service functions, CSQA does not solve problems in the UBSD, it identifies and manages problems. CSQA is a robust role, with the largest set of Key Work Processes in the UBSD. CSQA performs many of the functions traditionally associated with an Account Manager. Also, we have combined the roles of Customer Service and Quality Assurance further expanding the traditional function of Customer Service. This dramatic shift in the scope of the role is why we refer to it simply as CSQA. It will be easier if you use the name CSQA to avoid the confusion that is created by using the phrase Customer Service and Quality Assurance.

CSQA performs the following:

1. CSQA transforms the new Customer prospect's *request*

Figure 12.1

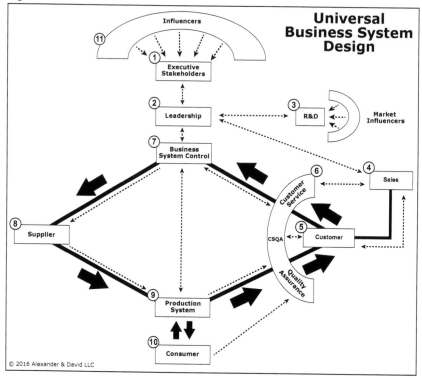

for proposal and quantitative *Customer objectives* into an *accepted contract* and *Customer contract requirements* delivered to BSC.

2. CSQA transforms a contracted *Customer's order objectives* into *order requirements* delivered to BSC.

3. CSQA transforms the *Measurement System Design data* from the Work System into *confirmation* to the Customer that the Work System is meeting requirements, or an *expanded contract* wherein the Work System is delivering expanded value to the Customer.

4. CSQA transforms *problems* impacting the Customer into *resolutions*.

ROLE & RESPONSIBILITIES

Role:

The role of CSQA is the Customer's gateway to the Work System. CSQA protects the Work System from the waste created when the Customer circumvents quantitative alignment and enters the Work System.

> *When the Customer tells the Work System "how" to do what it does, the Work System loses money. When the Work System chooses "how" to meet the Customer's requirements, the Work System makes money.*

CSQA keeps the Customer out of the Work System through Quantitative Alignment to the Customer's objectives (what the Executive Stakeholders or Customers want to accomplish with the help of the Work System). This process quantitatively confirms that the Work System processes are capable of meeting the Customer's objectives. Quantitative process capabilities aligned to meet the Customer's objectives is the only way to give the Customer the confidence necessary to keep them from entering the Work System and creating waste.

CSQA is responsible for delivering adequate supply to three internal UBSD customers: BSC, R&D, and Sales, and the external Customer. In order to meet this responsibility, CSQA depends on adequate delivery of supply from three internal suppliers: Sales, R&D, the Production System, and the external Customer.

Responsibilities:

- CSQA transforms Customer objectives from Sales into Customer requirements, and then aligns current Work System process capabilities with the Customer requirements to identify the Work System processes capable of meeting Customer requirements for contracts and orders.

- If current Work System processes are capable of meeting

Customer requirements, then CSQA produces and delivers a proposed contract to the Customer for approval.

- After the Customer approves a contract, CSQA on-boards the Customer by collaboratively designing a CCRP with the Customer and securing Customer acceptance of the CCRP. During on-boarding, CSQA also alerts R&D of a new contract, triggering R&D's creation of a qualified list of Suppliers.

- Once work has begun and orders are flowing through the Work System, CSQA regularly receives data from the Measurement System Design (MSD) and is alerted when the data indicates a problem. CSQA assesses the problem alert and decides whether or not to trigger the CCRP.

- Once CSQA triggers the CCRP, CSQA works with the Production System and the Customer to resolve the problem. If the problem cannot be resolved following the Response Plan, then CSQA sends the problem to R&D for remedy.

- If a problem cannot be solved, CSQA employs the Service Recovery to identify an external resource that meets the Customer's requirements and then refers the Customer to that resource. Service Recovery provides CSQA with a process for maintaining a positive relationship with a Customer despite the Work System's inability to meet requirements.

- After Service Recovery, if the Customer cancels the contract, then CSQA forwards the Customer contact information to Sales to manage until another contract opportunity is identified. If the contract is retained, then CSQA continues to manage the Customer.

CSQA KEY WORK PROCESSES (KWP)

CSQA is responsible for eighteen Key Work Processes (KWP's).

1. *06010E*
Transform a Request for Proposal with Customer Objectives into Customer Requirements

CSQA transforms a *request for proposal with Customer objectives* into *Customer requirements*.

Supplier: Sales

Inputs: Request for proposal with Customer objectives

Process: Transform a request for proposal with Customer objectives into Customer requirements

Outputs: Customer requirements

Customer: CSQA

2. *06020E*
Transform Customer Requirements and Processes into a Decision Identifying Capable Processes

CSQA transforms *Customer requirements* and *current Customer processes* into a *decision* identifying capable processes.

Supplier: CSQA and Work System Process Library

Inputs: Customer requirements and current Customer processes

Process: Transform Customer requirements and current Customer processes into a decision identifying capable processes

Outputs: Capable Customer processes with requirements and incapable Customer processes.

Customer: CSQA or R&D

3. *06030E*
Transform Capable Processes with Customer Requirements into a Contract Proposal

CSQA transforms *capable Customer processes with*

Figure 12.2

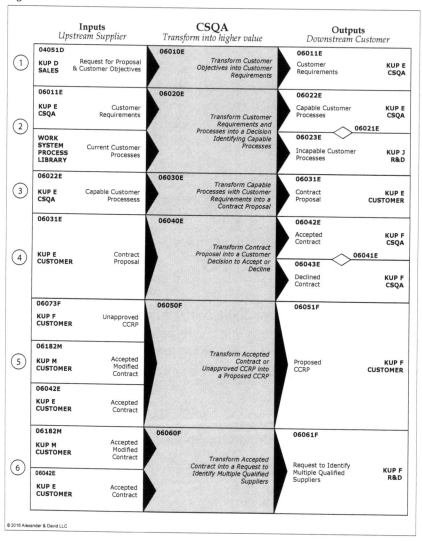

Customer requirements into a *contract proposal*.

Supplier: CSQA

Inputs: Capable Customer processes with Customer requirements

Process: Transform capable Customer processes with Customer requirements into a contract proposal

Outputs: Contract proposal

Customer: Customer

4. **06040E**
Transform Contract Proposal into a Customer Decision to Accept or Decline

CSQA transforms the *contract proposal* into a Customer *decision to accept or decline.*

Supplier: Customer

Inputs: Contract proposal

Process: Transform contract proposal into a Customer decision to accept or decline

Outputs: An accepted contract or a declined contract

Customer: CSQA

5. **06050F**
Transform Accepted Contract or Unapproved CCRP into a Proposed CCRP

CSQA transforms an *accepted contract, accepted modified contract* or *unapproved CCRP* into a *proposed Communication and Conflict Resolution Plan (CCRP).*

Supplier: Customer

Inputs: Accepted contract, accepted modified contract, or unapproved CCRP

Process: Transform an accepted new or modified contract into a proposed Communication and Conflict Resolution Plan (CCRP)

Outputs: Proposed CCRP

Customer: Customer

6. **06060F**
Transform Accepted Contract into a Request to Identify Multiple Qualified Suppliers

CSQA transforms an *accepted contract* or *accepted modified contract* into a *request to identify multiple qualified suppliers.*

Supplier: Customer

Inputs: Accepted new or modified contract

Process: Transform accepted new or modified contract into a request to identify multiple qualified Suppliers

Outputs: Request to identify multiple qualified Suppliers

Customer: R&D

7. **06070F**
   Transform Proposed CCRP into a Customer Decision to Approve or Decline
   CSQA transforms the *proposed Communication and Conflict Resolution Plan (CCRP)* into a *Customer decision* to approve or decline the CCRP.

   Supplier: Customer

   Inputs: Proposed CCRP

   Process: Transform proposed CCRP into a Customer decision to approve or decline the proposed CCRP

   Outputs: An approved CCRP or unapproved CCRP

   Customer: CSQA

8. **06080H**
   Transform Customer Order Objectives into Customer Order Requirements
   CSQA transforms *Customer order objectives* into *Customer order requirements.*

   Supplier: Customer

   Inputs: Customer order objectives

   Process: Transform Customer order objectives into Customer order requirements

   Outputs: Customer order requirements

Figure 12.3

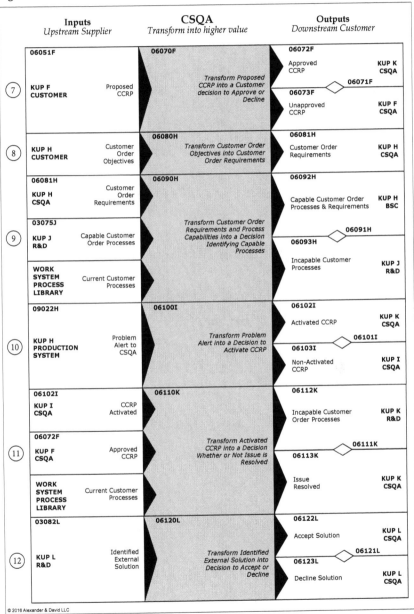

Customer: CSQA

9. 06090H
Transform Customer Order Requirements and Processes into a Decision Identifying Capable Processes

CSQA transforms *Customer order requirements, current Customer processes* and *capable Customer order processes* into a *decision* that identifies capable processes.

Supplier: CSQA, R&D and Work System Process Library

Inputs: Customer order requirements, capable Customer processes, and current Customer processes

Process: Transform Customer order requirements, capable Customer processes and current Customer processes into a decision identifying capable Customer order processes with requirements

Outputs: Capable Customer order processes with Customer order requirements or incapable Customer order processes

Customer: BSC and R&D

10. 06100I
Transform Problem Alert to CSQA into Decision to Activate CCRP

CSQA transforms a *problem alert to CSQA* into a *decision* whether to activate CCRP.

Supplier: Production System

Inputs: Problem alert to CSQA

Process: Transform problem alert to CSQA into a decision whether or not to activate CCRP

Outputs: Activated CCRP or non-activated CCRP

Customer: CSQA

11. 06110K
Transform Activated CCRP into a Decision Whether or Not Issue is Resolved

CSQA transforms *activated CCRP* into a *decision* whether or not the issue is resolved.

Supplier: CSQA

Inputs: Activated CCRP

Process: Transform activated CCRP into a decision whether or not the issue is resolved

Outputs: Incapable Customer processes or issue resolved

Customer: R&D or CSQA

12. 06120L
Transform Identified External Solution into Customer Decision to Accept or Decline

CSQA transforms the *identified external solution* into a *Customer decision* to accept or decline.

Supplier: R&D

Inputs: Identified external solution

Process: Transform identified external solution into a decision to accept or decline

Outputs: An accepted offer or a decline offer

Customer: CSQA

13. 06130L
Transform Accepted Solution into a Retained or Lost Contract

CSQA transforms *accepted solution* into a *retained or lost contract.*

Supplier: CSQA

Inputs: Accepted offer

Process: Transform accepted offer into a decision whether or not contract is lost

Outputs: Lost contract or contract retained

Customer: Sales or CSQA

14. 06140H
Transform MSD Data into an Opportunity to Confirm or Increase Value

CSQA transforms *Measurement System Design data* into an *opportunity to confirm or increase value.*

Supplier: Production system

Inputs: Measurement System Design data

Process: Transform MSD data into opportunity to confirm or increase value

Outputs: Opportunity to confirm or increase value

Customer: CSQA

15. 06150M
Transform Opportunity to Confirm or Increase Value into Report

CSQA transforms the *opportunity to confirm or increase value* into a *report.*

Supplier: CSQA

Inputs: Opportunity to confirm or increase value

Process: Transform opportunity to confirm or increase value into a report

Outputs: Report

Customer: Customer

16. 06160M
Transform Report into Decision to Approve or Decline Value Increase

CSQA transforms the *report* into a *decision* to approve value increase.

Figure 12.4

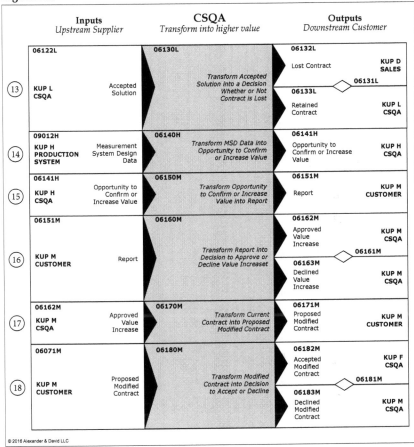

© 2016 Alexander & David LLC

Supplier: Customer

Inputs: Report

Process: Transform report into decision to approve value increase or not

Outputs: Approved value increase or declined value increase

Customer: CSQA

17. 06170M

Transform Current Contract into Proposed Modified Contract

CSQA transforms the *current contract* into a *proposed modified contract.*

Supplier: CSQA

Inputs: Approved value increase

Process: Transform current contract into a proposed modified contract

Outputs: Proposed modified contract

Customer: Customer

18. 06180M

Transform Proposed Modified Contract into Decision to Accept or Decline Contract

CSQA transforms the *proposed modified contract* into a *decision* to accept contract.

Supplier: Customer

Inputs: Proposed modified contract

Process: Transform proposed modified contract into a decision to accept or decline

Outputs: Accepted modified contract or declined modified contract

Customer: CSQA

13
Research & Development (R&D)

DESCRIPTION

The Research & Development (R&D) Key Work System focuses singularly on business and Customer processes.

When a current, stable process—narrow variation—is incapable of meeting Customer or business requirements then the requirements and the incapable processes are sent to R&D for remedy. Also, when a current, stable process with defined capabilities fails repeatedly despite implementing a Response Plan, then the process is sent to R&D for remedy.

One of the biggest challenges when implementing Customer-Supplier Relationships and the UBSD is becoming comfortable with allowing processes to fail. In the current state of most organizations, exceptional individuals employ exceptional effort in order to "catch" processes that fail and remedy them at the point of failure. This method of managing process failure is waste. The moment we agree to manage process failure at the point of failure,

Figure 13.1

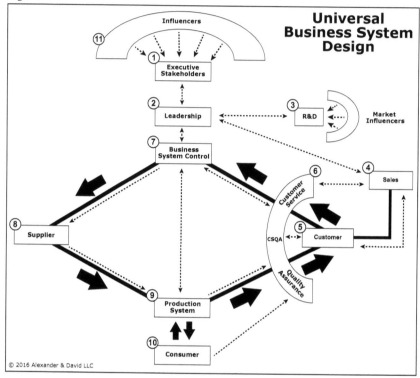

we are creating a problem-solving process outside of R&D with the primary responsibility of rescuing ineffective processes rather than fixing the processes. This approach perpetuates the continued use of ineffective processes.

> *Processes must be allowed to fail*
> *in order to identify and reduce waste.*

ROLE & RESPONSIBILITIES

Role:

The role of R&D in the UBSD is to ensure business processes are capable of meeting Executive Stakeholder business requirements, and Customer processes are capable of meeting Customer requirements.

When a process is determined to be incapable, it is sent to R&D. R&D transforms the incapable process into a capable process or designs a new capable process.

R&D also monitors the organization's markets to identify the requirements of prospective Customers and the future requirements of all Customers—current and prospective—within the organization's target markets.

R&D is responsible for delivering adequate supply to five internal UBSD customers: Leadership, BSC, CSQA, Sales, and the Production System. In order to meet this responsibility, R&D depends on adequate delivery of supply from six internal suppliers: Leadership, BSC, CSQA, Sales, the Production System, and the external Customer.

Responsibilities:

- R&D receives business requirements from Leadership and aligns them with current R&D business process capabilities to identify the R&D processes capable of meeting the business requirements. If one or more current R&D business processes are determined to be incapable of meeting the business requirements, they are sent to R&D for remedy.

- Once capable processes have been identified, R&D transforms the business requirements into business specifications and delivers them to R&D.

- R&D collects market data to identify market objectives and transforms them into market requirements. R&D then aligns the market requirements with current Customer process capabilities to identify the Customer processes capable of meeting the market requirements. If one or more current Customer processes are determined to be incapable of meeting the market requirements, they are sent to R&D for remedy.

- Whenever a Key Work System identifies an incapable process, the process and the requirements are both sent to R&D for remedy. For the Production System, when the

Response Plan is unable to remedy a process failure, the process is sent to R&D. R&D transforms the incapable processes and requirements into proposals to build or redesign and submits these proposals to Leadership for approval. If Leadership approves the proposals, then R&D transforms the incapable processes into a capable process and delivers the new or redesigned processes to the appropriate Key Work System for immediate implementation.

- During *KUP F: Customer On-Boarding*, R&D identifies a list of multiple qualified suppliers to support the Customer contract in preparation for future orders. R&D delivers this list to BSC, ensuring BSC is prepared for *KUP G: Supplier Selection*.

- During *KUP L: Service Recovery*, R&D conducts research to identify an alternative external solution to meet Customer requirements. R&D delivers this solution to CSQA for delivery to the Customer.

R&D KEY WORK PROCESSES (KWP)

R&D is responsible for eight Key Work Processes (KWP's).

1. *03010B*

Transform R&D Business Requirements and Current R&D Business Processes into a Decision Identifying Capable Processes

R&D transforms *R&D business requirements* and *current R&D business processes* into a *decision* that identifies capable processes.

Supplier: Leadership and R&D Process Library

Inputs: R&D business requirements and current R&D business processes

Process: Transform R&D business requirements and current R&D business processes into a decision identifying capable processes

Figure 13.2

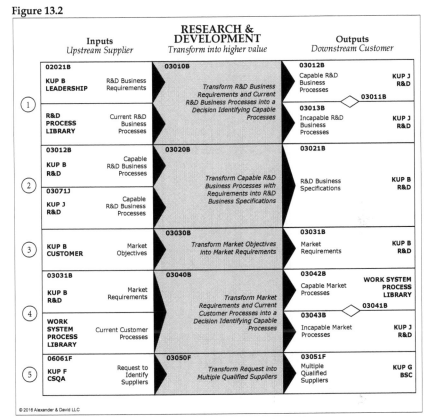

RESEARCH & DEVELOPMENT
Transform into higher value

① Inputs — Upstream Supplier		Outputs — Downstream Customer

© 2016 Alexander & David LLC

Outputs: Capable R&D business processes with requirements and incapable R&D business process capabilities

Customer: R&D

2. 03020B

Transform Capable R&D Business Processes with Requirements into R&D Business Specifications

R&D transforms *capable R&D business processes* with *R&D business requirements* into *R&D business specifications.*

Supplier: R&D

Inputs: Capable R&D business processes with R&D business requirements

Process: Transform capable R&D business processes

with R&D business requirements into R&D business
specifications

Outputs: R&D business specifications

Customer: R&D

3. ***03030B***

    Transform Market Objectives into Market Requirements

    R&D transforms *market objectives* into *market requirements*.

    Supplier: Customer

    Inputs: Market objectives

    Process: Transform market objectives into market
    requirements

    Outputs: Market requirements

    Customer: R&D

4. ***03040B***

    ***Transform Market Requirements and Current Customer
    Processes into a Decision Identifying Capable Processes***

    R&D transforms the *market requirements* and *current
    Customer processes* into a *decision* that identifies capable
    processes.

    Supplier: R&D and Work System Process Library

    Inputs: Market requirements and current Customer
    processes

    Process: Transform market requirements and current
    Customer processes into a decision identifying capable
    processes.

    Outputs: Capable Customer processes with requirements
    and incapable Customer processes

    Customer: R&D and Work System Process Library

5. ***03050F***

    Transform Request into Multiple Qualified Suppliers

    R&D transforms the *request to identify qualified Suppliers*

Figure 13.3

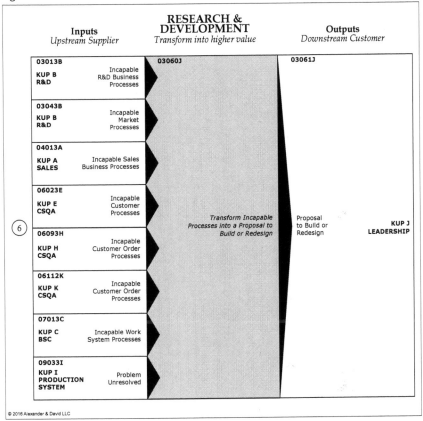

into a list of *multiple qualified Suppliers*.

Supplier: CSQA

Inputs: Request to identify Suppliers

Process: Transform request to identify Suppliers into multiple qualified Suppliers

Outputs: Multiple qualified Suppliers

Customer: BSC

6. *03060J*
Transform Incapable Processes into Proposal to Build or Redesign

R&D transforms *incapable processes* or *problems unresolved* into a *proposal to build or redesign*.

Supplier: R&D, Sales, CSQA, BSC and Production System

Inputs: Incapable processes and problems unresolved

Process: Transform incapable processes and problems unresolved into a proposal to build or redesign

Outputs: Proposal to build or redesign

Customer: Leadership

7. 03070J
Transform a Decision to Build into a Capable Process

R&D transforms the *decision to build* into a *capable process* or a *problem resolved*.

Supplier: Leadership

Inputs: Decision to build

Process: Transform a decision to build into a capable process or problem resolved

Outputs: Capable processes and problems resolved

Customer: R&D, Sales, Work System Process Library, CSQA, BSC and Production System

8. 03080L
Transform a Declined Contract into an Identified External Solution

R&D transforms a *declined contract* into a *decision* identifying whether or not an external solution exists.

Supplier: CSQA

Inputs: Declined contract

Process: Transform a declined contract into decision identifying whether or not an external solution exist

Outputs: External solution identified and no external solution identified

Customer: CSQA

Figure 13.3

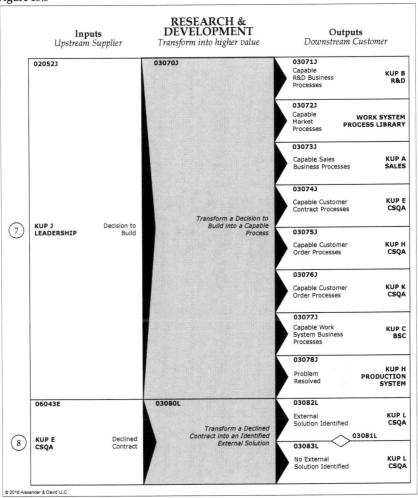

14
Business System Control (BSC)

DESCRIPTION

The Business System Control (BSC) Key Work System transforms *Customer requirements* and *business requirements* into *specifications*.

ROLE & RESPONSIBILTIES

Role:

The role of BSC in the UBSD is to transform requirements into specifications.

BSC serves two internal UBSD customers: Supplier and Production System. In order to meet this responsibility, BSC depends on adequate delivery of supply from four internal suppliers: Leadership, CSQA, R&D, and the Supplier.

Responsibilities:

- BSC receives business requirements from Leadership and

Figure 14.1

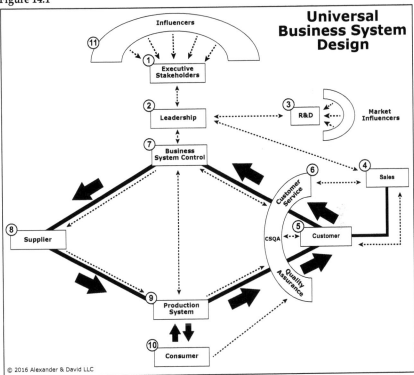

aligns them with current Work System business process capabilities to identify the business processes capable of meeting the business requirements. If one or more current Work System business processes are determined to be incapable of meeting the business requirements, they are sent to R&D for remedy.

- BSC transforms business requirements from Leadership and capable Work System business processes into business specifications for the Work System — the Supplier and Production System.

- BSC transforms Customer requirements from CSQA and capable Work System Customer processes into Customer specifications for the Work System.

BSC KEY WORK PROCESSES (KWP)

BSC is responsible for five Key Work Processes (KWP's).

1. 07010C
Transform Work System Business Requirements and Processes into a Decision Identifying Capable Business Processes

BSC transforms the *Work System business requirements* and *Work System business processes* into a *decision* that identifies capable business processes.

Supplier: Leadership

Inputs: Work System business requirements and Work System business processes

Process: Transform Work System business requirements and Work System business processes into a decision identifying capable Work System business processes

Outputs: Capable incapable Work System business processes with requirements or incapable Work System business processes

Customer: BSC and R&D

2. 07020C
Transform Work System Capable Business Processes with Requirements into Work System Business Specifications

BSC transforms *capable Work System business processes* with *Work System business requirements* into *Work System business specifications.*

Supplier: BSC and R&D

Inputs: Capable Work System business processes with Work System business requirements

Process: Transform capable Work System business processes with Work System business requirements into Work System business specifications

Figure 14.2

	Inputs *Upstream Supplier*	BUSINESS SYSTEM CONTROL *Transform into higher value*	Outputs *Downstream Customer*
1	**02031C** **KUP C LEADERSHIP** Work System Business Requirements	**07010C** *Transform Work System Business Requirements and Processes into a Decision Identifying Capable Business Processes*	**07012C** Capable Work System **KUP C** Business Processes **BSC** ◇ 07011C **07013C** Incapable Work System **KUP J** Business Processes **R&D**
2	**07012C** **KUP C** Capable Work System **BSC** Business Processes **03077J** **KUP J** Capable Work System **R&D** Business Processes	**07020C** *Transform Work System Capable Business Processes with Requirements into Work System Business Specifications*	**07021C** Work System **KUP H** Business **BSC** Specifications
3	**07021C** **KUP H** Work System **BSC** Business Specifications **06092H** **KUP H** Capable Processes **CSQA** & Customer Order Requirements	**07030H** *Transform Customer Order Requirements and Capable Customer Order Processes into Customer Order Specifications*	**07031H** Customer Order Specifications for **KUP G** Supplier **BSC** **07032H** **KUP H** Customer Order **PRODUCTION** Specifications for **SYSTEM** Production System
4	**07031H** **KUP G** Customer Order **BSC** Specifications **03051F** **KUP F** Multiple **R&D** Qualified Suppliers **07053G** **KUP G** **BSC** Decline Offer	**07040G** *Transform Customer Order Specifications, Multiple Qualified Suppliers and Decline Offer into Supplier Order Specifications*	**07041G** Supplier Order **KUP G** Specifications **SUPPLIER**
5	**08011G** **KUP G** Offer Process **SUPPLIER** Capabilities	**07050G** *Transform Supplier Offer Process Capabilities into a Decision to Accept or Decline*	**07052G** Accept Offer **KUP G** **BSC** ◇ 07051C **07053G** Decline Offer **KUP G** **BSC**
6	**07052G** **KUP G** **BSC** Accept Offer	**07060G** *Transform Accepted Offer into Order for Resources, Materials or Parts*	**07061G** Order for Resources, **KUP G** Materials or Parts **SUPPLIER**

Outputs: Work System business specifications

Customer: BSC

3. *07030H*

Transform Customer Order Requirements and Capable Customer Order Processes into Customer Order Specifications

BSC transforms the *Customer order requirements* and capable *Customer order processes* with *Customer order requirements* into *Customer order specifications* for the Supplier and Production System.

Supplier: BSC and CSQA

Inputs: Work System business specifications, capable Customer order processes with Customer order requirements

Process: Transform Work System Customer order specifications and capable Customer order processes with Customer order requirements into Customer order specifications

Outputs: Customer order specifications for Supplier and Production System

Customer: BSC and Production System

4. *07040G*

Transform Multiple Qualified Suppliers, Customer Order Specifications, and a Decline Offer into Supplier Order Specifications

BSC transforms *multiple qualified suppliers, Customer order specifications,* and a *decline offer* into Supplier specifications.

Supplier: BSC, Supplier, and R&D

Inputs: Multiple qualified suppliers, Customer order specifications and a decline offer

Process: Transforms transforms multiple qualified suppliers, Customer order specifications, and a decision to pass from a Supplier into Supplier specifications

Outputs: Supplier order specifications

Customer: Supplier

5. 07050G
Transform Supplier Offer Process Capabilities into a Decision to Accept or Decline

BSC transforms Supplier's *offer of process capabilities* into a *decision* to accept or decline.

Supplier: Supplier

Inputs: Offer of process capabilities

Process: Transform Supplier's offer of process capabilities into a decision to accept or decline.

Outputs: Accept offer or decline offer

Customer: BSC

6. 07060G
Transform Offer Process Capabilities into Order for Resources, Materials or Parts

BSC transforms Supplier's *offer of process capabilities* into a *decision* to accept or decline.

Supplier: Supplier

Inputs: Offer of process capabilities

Process: Transform Supplier's offer of process capabilities into a decision to accept or decline.

Outputs: Order for resources, materials or parts

Customer: BSC

15
Supplier

DESCRIPTION

The Supplier Key Work System encompasses both internal and external providers of resources, materials or parts specified by BSC to ensure adequate supply to the Production System to meet the Customer and business requirements. The Supplier transforms Customer order specifications from BSC into resources, materials or parts delivered to the Production System.

In many current state business systems, the Supplier uses the demand for its resources as leverage to dictate terms — they issue requirements to the Customer rather than responding to the requirements of Customers. For internal Suppliers, this dysfunction is promoted by the silos and competitive work team relationships created by traditional chain-of-command organizational hierarchy. It is further perpetuated by single source Supplier options wherein the Customer has only one Supplier option and must accept the terms of the Supplier or risk receiving inadequate supply. Toyota's Kaoru Ishikawa remedied the dysfunctional relationships between Customers and Suppliers with a simple set of rules.[15.2]

[15.2]*What is Total Quality Control? The Japanese Way*, Kaoru Ishikawa

Figure 15.1

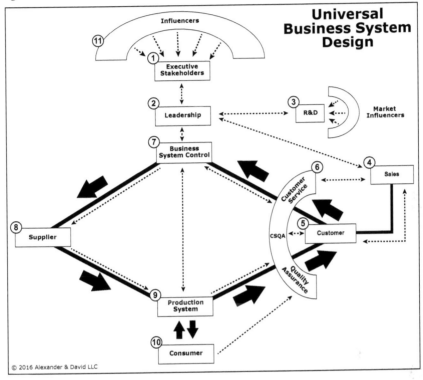

Ishikawa's rules for the Customer-Supplier Relationship are:

1. *The Customer must provide clear and sufficient requirements to the Supplier.*

2. *The Supplier must deliver adequate value to meet the requirements of the Customer.*

In the UBSD, the Supplier has two choices: *accept* or *pass*. The Supplier does not have the option to dictate terms to the Customer. For this to work, the Customer must have access to multiple Suppliers allowing the Customer to choose a Supplier that can meet requirements.

Any organization that dictates their internal customers use a single, internal supplier is fostering significant dysfunction and waste that consumes margins and jeopardizes the capability of the Production System to meet the external Customer requirements.

ROLE & RESPONSIBILITIES

Role:

The role of the Supplier in the UBSD is to transform Customer order specifications and business specifications into resources, materials or parts delivered to the Production System.

When BSC issues specifications to the Supplier during *KUP G: Supplier Selection*, the Supplier has only two possible responses: *accept* or *pass*. If the Supplier elects to pass, the Customer finds an alternative Supplier.

The decision to accept may be impacted by whether or not the Supplier has processes capable of meeting specifications. If the Supplier does not have capable processes, the Supplier must decide whether to *build* or *pass*. The decision to build or pass also applies to the Supplier's access to resources, materials and parts, and the Supplier's capacity.

The Supplier is responsible for delivering adequate supply to one internal customer: Production System. In order to meet this responsibility, the Supplier depends on adequate delivery of supply from one internal supplier: BSC.

Responsibilities:

- The Supplier receives Supplier order specifications from BSC and delivers to the Production System the resources, materials or parts that meet Supplier order specifications.

- If the Supplier's processes are incapable of meeting the specifications, the Supplier either elects to build or pass. A build decision indicates the Supplier will design a new process or redesign an existing process in order to meet specifications.

SUPPLIER KEY WORK PROCESSES (KWP)

Supplier is responsible for five Key Work Processes (KWP's).

1. *08010G*
Transform Supplier Order Specifications into an Offer of Process Capabilities

The Supplier transforms the *Supplier order specifications* into

Figure 15.2

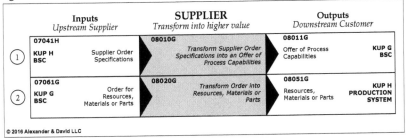

an *offer of process capabilities.*

Supplier: BSC

Inputs: Supplier order specifications

Process: Transform transforms the Supplier order specifications into an offer of process capabilities

Outputs: Offer of process capabilities

Customer: Supplier

2. 08020G
Transform Order into Resources, Materials or Parts

The Supplier transforms an *order* for resources, materials or parts into *resources, materials or parts*

Supplier: Supplier

Inputs: Order for resources, materials or parts

Process: Transform an order for resources, materials or parts into resources, materials or parts

Outputs: Resources, materials or parts

Customer: Production System

16
Production System

DESCRIPTION

The Production System Key Work System is where the organizations product is produced or its service is delivered. It is not defined by brick and mortar—it can be online or on the phone, on a mobile device or on traditional TV.

The Production System usually consists of many processes working together to produce a product or deliver a service. Business performance improvement has focused on the Production System for more than 50 years. The Production System continues to be the primary area of focus for improvement for many organizations and, in the UBSD, it continues to be a critical part of the business system—but it is not the only part.

In the UBSD, the Production System is one of seven Key Work Systems that work together in the same way the Production System's Key Work Processes work together. Business performance improvement is not limited to the Production System—it is applied to the entire business system.

The history of focus on the Production System has created numerous innovations that have sustained organizations in

Figure 16.1

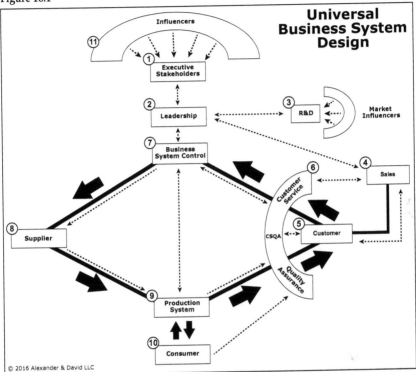

dynamic and highly competitive markets. The learning from this work has identified three critical conditions that must be present in order for the Production System to be effective and sustainable:

1. ***Adequate Supply and Capacity*** – Supply must be available when and where the Production System requires it; and the Production System must have adequate capacity. Both factors directly impact throughput.

2. ***Stable, Repeatable and Reproducible Processes*** – The Production System cannot be disrupted by variation. The roles outside the black diamond in Figure 16.1 cannot be allowed to introduce variation into the Production System. Variation destroys throughput.

3. *R&D Cannot be Performed in the Production System* — In many organizations, this is how the Production System responds to variation. When the Production System maintains unstable processes with problem-solving — and problem-solving in the Production System destroys throughput.

ROLE & RESPONSIBILTIES

Role:

The role of the Production System in the UBSD is to transform *Customer order specifications* into *finished products or services* delivered to the Consumer.

The Consumer is not always the Customer. The Consumer is *always* the recipient or consumer of the product or service. The Customer is *always* the payer. In many cases, they are the same and, in others, they are different (e.g. healthcare wherein the patient is the Consumer and the insurance company, employer or government is the Customer).

The most important distinction, as far as the UBSD is concerned, is the Work System must meet Customer requirements, not Consumer requirements. It is the Customer who pays the piper and calls the tune, not the Consumer. Members of the Production System can lose sight of this distinction and confuse the Consumer with the Customer, resulting in the Production System working to meet Consumer requirements at the expense of Customer requirements.

The Production System is responsible for delivering adequate supply to one internal UBSD customer: CSQA; and one external customer: Consumer.

Responsibilities:

- The Production System transforms resources, materials or parts from the Supplier; Production System capacity; and capable Customer processes into finished product or services delivered to the Consumer.

- The Production System collects and distributes Measurement System Design data to CSQA.

- The Production System transforms a problem and the Response Plan into a decision whether or not the problem is resolved. If unresolved, the Production System sends the problem to R&D.

PRODUCTION SYSTEM KEY WORK PROCESSES (KWP)

The Production System is responsible for three Key Work Processes (KWP's).

1. 09010H
Transform Customer Order Specifications; Resources, Materials or Parts; and Problems Resolved into Finished Products or Services

The Production System transforms *Customer order specifications* for the Production System; *resources, materials or parts*; and *problems resolved* into finished product or services delivered to the Consumer.

Supplier: BSC, Supplier, and Production System

Inputs: Customer order specifications; resources, materials or parts; and problems unresolved

Process: Transform Customer order specifications for the Production System; resources, materials or parts; and problems resolved into finished product or services

Outputs: Finished products or services, Measurement System Design data

Customer: Consumer and Production System

2. 09020H
Transform MSD Data into Problem Alert or No Action Required

The Production System transforms the *Measurement System Design data* into a *decision* identifying a whether ot not a

Figure 16.2

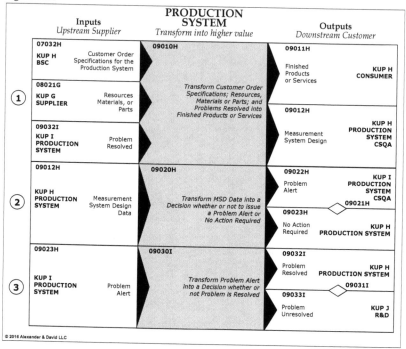

problem alert should be issued.

Supplier: Production System

Inputs: Measurement System Design data

Process: Transform MSD data into a decision whether or not a problem alert should be issued

Outputs: Problem alert and no action required

Customer: CSQA and Production System

3. 09030I

Transform Problem Alert and Response Plan into a Decision Whether or Not Problem is Resolved

The Production System transforms the *problem alert* into a *decision* whether or not the problem is resolved.

Supplier: BSC

Inputs: Problem alert

Process: Transform the problem alert into a decision whether or not the problem is resolved

Outputs: Problem resolved or problem unresolved

Customer: Production System and R&D

Part 4
Key UBSD Processes

INTRODUCTION TO KEY UBSD PROCESSES

In Part 4, we provide process design details for the thirteen Key UBSD Processes (KUP).

In Figure P4.1, you see the key parts of the UBSD and their relationships. A KUP is a process that A) transforms *inputs* into *higher value outputs*, B) produces outputs that are critical to throughput for the organizations core functions — planning, sales, production, problem response, and upsell as shown in Figure P4.2

Figure P4.1

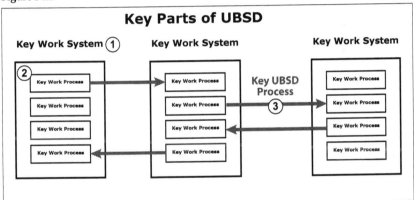

Figure P4.2

Label	Title	Type	Chapter
KUP A	Sales Business Plan	Planning	17
KUP B	R&D Business Plan	Planning	18
KUP C	Work System Business Plan	Planning	19
KUP D	New Customer Opportunity	Sales	20
KUP E	New Customer Engagement	Sales	21
KUP F	Customer Onboarding	Sales	22
KUP G	Supplier Selection	Production	23
KUP H	Product Order & Delivery	Production	24
KUP I	Problem Response Plan	Problem Response	25
KUP J	New Process or Redesign	Problem Response	26
KUP K	CCRP	Problem Response	27
KUP L	Service Recovery	Problem Response	28
KUP M	Report Out	Upsell	29

and C) is a sequence of activities linking multiple *Key Work Processes* in multiple *Key Work Systems*.

WHY IS THIS IMPORTANT?

For most readers, the following thirteen chapters may appear to be a confusing set of process diagrams and descriptive narrative. However, if you look closer and take the time to understand them, you will discover they provide a powerful blueprint for achieving exceptional business performance.

Customer-Supplier Relationships and the UBSD do not design your solution, they make it *effective* and *sustainable*. Mission Simple provides the rails your vision rides on. It ensures you achieve your vision with the lowest possible investment and risk. These thirteen chapters give you the blueprint for the rails.

We have provided these chapters as a playbook you can follow to implement Mission Simple in your organization. In Chapter 30, we discuss implementation in more detail.

HOW DO I USE THE KUP'S?

Each KUP is *universal* — regardless of whether your organization manufactures products, provides services or is a not-for-profit. It is important to avoid confusing the unique nature of your *business* and the universal nature of your *business system* — your business is unique, your business system is universal.

In *Parts 1 & 2 Summary & Review,* we describe the simple rule of "play your position." In the KUP's, this rule is expanded to "stay in your swim lane." The *Key Work Systems* describe your position in the business system, and their *Key Work Processes* describe the work you *should* and *should not* do. The *Key UBSD Processes* describe the most effective way to work with other *Key Work Systems* to ensure the organization achieves exceptional business performance.

HOW TO READ THE CHAPTERS

Each chapter follows the structure below.

1. **Description** — The *description* section of each chapter

describes the value the process delivers by transforming inputs into higher value outputs. The description identifies the multiple Key Work Systems that participate in the KUP.

2. **Input**—The *input* section describes the primary inputs and triggers for the KUP. A trigger is an input that "triggers" the start of the KUP. The KUP cannot begin until it receives a trigger input.

3. **Process**—The *process* section describes the multiple Key Work Processes in the KUP. All KUP's are comprised of multiple KWP's from at least two Key Work Systems.

4. **Output**—The *output* section describes the primary outputs and terminus for the KUP. There are two types of KUP outputs: *throughput outputs* and *problem outputs*. Throughput outputs contribute to throughput. Problem outputs are barriers to throughput and require remedy to ensure effective throughput. A terminus describes the action that ends the KUP.

5. **Cross-Functional Swim Lane Diagram**—The KUP's are illustrated using a classic *cross-functional swim lane diagram* shown in Figure P4.3. The diagrams illustrate each of the participating Key Work Systems as *swim lanes* and how the work flows from one Key Work System to another. Most importantly, the swim lane diagrams display the work each swim lane is responsible for to ensure the effectiveness of the KUP.

6. **Step-by-Step Work Flow**—In addition to the swim lane diagrams, each chapter provides a *step-by-step work flow* narrative description of the KUP, describing the inputs, processes, outputs and decisions.

THE LANGUAGE OF THE KUP'S

A casual read of the KUP chapters will deliver little value to you or your efforts to improve your organization because the text is in a

Figure P4.3

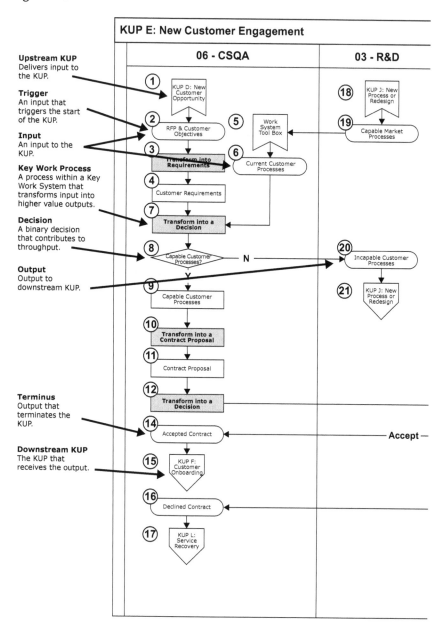

foreign language. If you don't know the language of the KUP's, the words and phrases will appear arbitrary and meaningless.

We want to stress that the language of the KUP is precise – the words and their descriptions are not qualitative but quantitative. If you do not fully understand them, you will not be able to understand the importance of what is being described. Because we use words and phrases that appear familiar, it is easy to assume you understand them. You may understand them in their broad qualitative context, but in the UBSD they have a precise and quantitative meaning. The language of the KUP's leaves no room for subjective judgement. Without this precision, it is impossible to achieve stable, repeatable and reproducible processes.

We have provided a glossary below that applies to the KUP's. Take the time to read through the glossary. Invest time on the language. At first, this may seem like a burden, but once you have mastered the language, the value of the KUP's opens up for you.

We also recommend you place a marker on the glossary page and use it as a quick reference while reading through the KUP chapters.

INTENTIONAL REWORK LOOPS

There are few intentional rework loops in the KUP's. The purpose of these rework loops is to avoid losing the significant value of completing the primary process – the value outweighs the potential disruption of the rework loop.

THE KUP GLOSSARY

Business Objectives — A *business* objective is a type of objective that quantitatively defines what the *Executive Stakeholder* wants to accomplish with the help of the Work System. Note that it does not tell the Work System what to produce. Business objectives are inputs to the Work System and originate outside of the Work System.

Business Requirements — A *business* requirement is a type of requirement that quantitatively defines the outputs that must be produced to achieve the *Executive Stakeholder* objectives. Business requirements are produced within the Work System in response to business objectives.

Capable Processes — A *capable* process is a type of process whose capabilities are *capable* of meeting the business requirements.

Incapable Processes — An *incapable* process is a type of process whose *process* capabilities are *incapable* of meeting the business requirements.

Key Performance Indicators (KPI's) — KPI's are objectives expressed as quantitative measures that track the Work System's progress toward achieving what the Executive Stakeholders or Customers want to accomplish. Business KPI's are determined by the objectives of the Executive Stakeholder.

Market — The Market is defined as *all* of the organization's current and prospective Customers.

Process Capabilities — Process capabilities define the range of results a process produces over time. Process capabilities are documented in a control chart.

Problem — A problem is defined as a process with defined capabilities that begins producing multiple results outside of its established control limits. For example, let's say the "time-to-finish" capabilities for a process ranges from five to fifteen minutes. A single result outside of that range is not a problem. However, a number of results outside of that range indicates a problem.

Problem Alert — A problem alert is a notification to the Production System and CSQA that a process is experiencing a problem.

Problem Output — A problem output is a barrier to effective throughput and requires a remedy to restore effective throughput.

Problem Resolved — A problem resolved defines a process that has returned to producing results within established control limits.

Problem Unresolved — A problem unresolved defines a process that continues to produce multiple results beyond established control limits.

Throughput Output — A throughput output is an output that contributes to effective business system throughput.

Quantitative Alignment — A process that ensures the Supplier and Work System process capabilities are *capable* of meeting the requirements of the Executive Stakeholders.

17
KUP A: Sales Business Plan

DESCRIPTION

KUP A: Sales Business Plan transforms *Sales business objectives* into *Sales business specifications*.

KUP A involves three Key Work Systems shown as three distinct swim lanes in the cross-functional swim lane diagram shown in 17.1:

1. *Leadership (02)*
2. *Sales (04)*
3. *R&D (03)*

INPUT

The primary input and trigger of KUP A is *Sales business objectives*. KUP A does not begin until the *Sales business objectives* are received by Leadership.

Figure 17.1

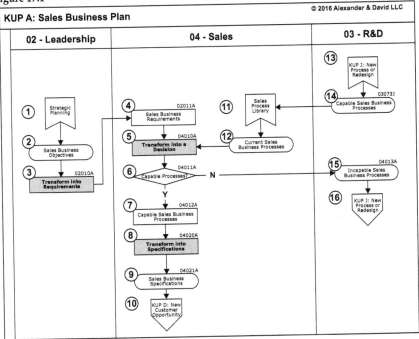

PROCESS

KUP A consists of three Key Work Processes:

02010A
Transform Sales Business Objectives into Sales Business Requirements

Leadership transforms *Sales business objectives* into *Sales business requirements.*

04010A
Transform Sales Business Requirements and Current Sales Business Processes into a Decision Identifying Capable Processes

Sales transforms *Sales business requirements* and *current Sales business processes* into a *decision* that identifies capable processes.

04020A
Transform Capable Sales Business Processes & Requirements into Sales Business Specifications

Sales transforms *capable Sales business processes* and *Sales business requirements* into *Sales business specifications.*

OUTPUTS

The throughput output and terminus of KUP A is *Sales business specifications.* Work ends when the *Sales business specifications* are delivered to KUP D. The problem output of KUP A is *incapable Sales business processes.*

STEP-BY-STEP WORK FLOW

KUP A: Sales Business Plan consists of 16 individual steps. The numbers for each step correspond to Figures 17.1.

1. **Strategic Planning**

    Strategic Planning is an upstream process that delivers *Sales business objectives* to KUP A.

2. **Sales Business Objectives**

    Sales business objectives is the throughput output of Strategic Planning.

3. **02010A**
    Transform Sales Business Objectives into Sales Business Requirements

    Leadership transforms *Sales business objectives* into *Sales business requirements.*

4. **02011A**
    Sales Business Requirements

    Sales business requirements is a throughput output of KWP 02010A.

5. *04010A*
   Transform Sales Business Requirements and Current Sales Business Processes into a Decision Identifying Capable Processes

   Sales transforms *Sales business requirements* and *Sales business process capabilities* into a *decision* that identifies capable processes.

6. *04011A*
   Capable Processes?

   Sales decides whether or not *current process capabilities* can meet the *Sales business requirements*.

7. *04012A*
   Capable Sales Business Processes

   Capable Sales business processes is the throughput output of Key Work Process 04010A.

8. *04020A*
   Transform Capable Sales Business Processes & Requirements into Sales Business Specifications

   Sales transforms *capable Sales business processes* and *Sales business requirements* into *Sales business specifications*.

9. *04021A*
   Sales Business Specifications

   Sales business specifications is the throughput output of Key Work Process 04020A.

10. **KUP D: New Customer Opportunity**

    KUP D is a downstream KUP that receives the *Sales business specifications* from Key Work Process 04020A.

11. **Sales Process Library**

    The Sales Process Library contains the existing inventory of *current Sales business processes*.

12. Current Sales Business Processes

Current Sales business processes is the throughput output of the Sales Process Library.

13. KUP J: New Process or Redesign

KUP J is an upstream KUP that delivers *capable Sales business processes* to KUP A.

14. 03073J
Capable Sales Business Processes

Capable Sales business processes is the throughput output of KUP J.

15. 04013A
Incapable Sales Business Processes

Incapable Sales business processes is the problem output of Key Work Process 04010A.

16. KUP J: New Process or Redesign

KUP J is a downstream KUP that receives *incapable Sales business processes* from Key Work Process 04010A.

18
KUP B: R&D Business Plan

DESCRIPTION

KUP B: R&D Business Plan transforms *R&D business objectives R&D business specifications* – and transforms *market objectives* into *capable Customer processes*.

KUP B involves four Key Work Systems shown as four distinct swim lanes in the cross-functional swim lane diagram shown in Figure 18.1.

1. *Leadership (02)*
2. *R&D (03)*
3. *CSQA (06)*
4. *Customer (05)*

INPUT

The primary inputs and triggers of KUP B are *R&D business*

Figure 18.1

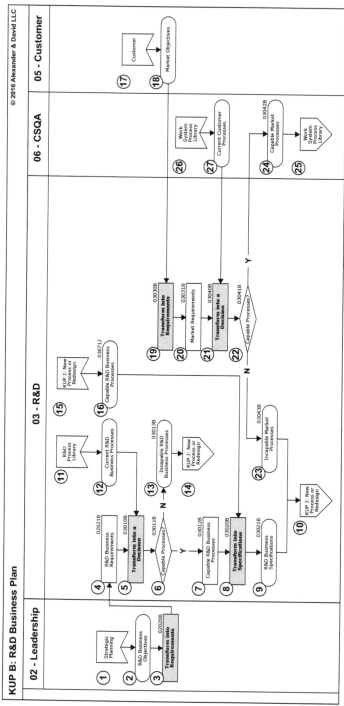

objectives and *market objectives*. KUP B does not begin until *R&D business objectives* are received by Leadership.

PROCESS

KUP B consists of five Key Work Processes:

02020B
Transform R&D Business Objectives into R&D Business Requirements

Leadership transforms *R&D business objectives* into *R&D business requirements*.

03010B
Transform R&D Business Requirements and Current R&D Business Processes into a Decision Identifying Capable Processes

R&D transforms *R&D business requirements* and *current R&D business processes* into a *decision* that identifies capable processes.

03020B
Transform Capable R&D Business Processes with Requirements into R&D Business Specifications

R&D transforms *capable R&D business processes* with *R&D business requirements* into *R&D business specifications*.

03030B
Transform Market Objectives into Market Requirements

R&D transforms *market objectives* into *market requirements*.

03040B
Transform Market Requirements and Current Customer Processes into a Decision Identifying Capable Processes

R&D transforms *market requirements* and *current Customer processes* into a *decision* that identifies capable processes.

OUTPUTS

The throughput outputs and terminus of KUP B is *R&D business specifications*. Work ends when the *R&D business specifications* are delivered to KUP J. The problem outputs of KUP B are *incapable R&D business processes* and *incapable market processes*.

STEP-BY-STEP WORK FLOW

KUP B: R&D Business Plan consists of 27 individual steps. The numbers correspond to Figure 18.1.

1. **Strategic Planning**

    Strategic Planning is an upstream process that delivers *R&D business objectives* to KUP B.

2. **R&D Business Objectives**

    R&D business objectives is the throughput output of Strategic Planning.

3. **02020B**

    Transform R&D Business Objectives into R&D Business Requirements

    Leadership transforms *R&D business objectives* into *R&D business requirements*.

4. **02021B**

    R&D Business Requirements

    R&D business objectives is the throughput output of Key Work Process 02020B.

5. **03010B**

    Transform R&D Business Requirements and Current R&D Business Processes into a Decision Identifying Capable Processes

    R&D transforms *R&D business requirements* and *current R&D business processes* into a *decision* that identifies capable processes.

6. **03011B**

    Capable R&D Business Processes?

    R&D decides whether or not *current R&D business processes* can meet *R&D business requirements*.

7. **03012B**

    Capable R&D Business Processes

    Capable R&D business processes is the throughput output of Key Work Process 3010B.

8. **03020B**
   Transform Capable R&D Business Processes with Requirements into R&D Business Specifications

   R&D transforms *capable R&D business processes* with *R&D business requirements* into *R&D business specifications*.

9. **03021B**
   R&D Business Specifications

   R&D business specifications is the throughput output of Key Work Process 3020B.

10. **KUP J: New Process or Redesign**

    KUP J is the downstream KUP that receives the *R&D business specifications* from Key Work Process 03020B.

11. **R&D Process Library**

    The R&D Process Library contains the existing inventory of *current R&D processes*.

12. **Current R&D Business Processes**

    Current R&D business processes is the throughput output of the R&D Process Library.

13. **03013B**
    Incapable R&D Business Processes

    Incapable R&D business processes is the problem output of Key Work Process 3010B.

14. **KUP J: New Process or Redesign**

    KUP J is a downstream KUP that receives *incapable R&D business processes* from Key Work Process 03010B.

15. **KUP J: New Process or Redesign**

    KUP J is an upstream KUP that delivers *capable R&D business processes* to Key Work Process 03020B.

16. **03071J**
    Capable R&D Business Processes

    Capable R&D business processes is the throughput output of the KUP J.

17. Customer

Customer is an upstream process that delivers *market objectives* to KUP J.

18. Market Objectives

Market objectives is the throughput output of the KUP J.

19. 03030B

Transform Market Objectives into Market Requirements

R&D transforms *market objectives* into *market requirements*.

20. 03031B

Market Requirements

Market requirements is the throughput output of the Key Work Process 03030B.

21. 03040B

Transform Market Requirements and Current Customer Processes into a Decision Identifying Capable Processes

R&D transforms *market requirements* and *current Customer processes* into a *decision* that identifies capable processes.

22. 03041B

Capable Market Processes?

R&D decides whether or not the *current Customer process capabilities* are capable of meeting *market requirements*.

23. 03043B

Incapable Market Processes

Incapable market processes is the problem output of the Key Work Process 03040B.

24. 03042B

Capable Market Processes

Capable market processes is the throughput output of the Key Work Process 03040B.

25. Work System Process Library

The Work System Process Library is the downstream Customer for *capable market processes*.

26. Work System Process Library

The Work System Process Library is the upstream Supplier of *current Customer processes*.

27. Current Customer Processes

Current Customer processes is the throughput output of the Work System Process Library.

19
KUP C: Work System Business Plan

DESCRIPTION

KUP C: Work System Business Plan transforms *Work System business objectives* into *Work System business specifications*.

KUP C involves three Key Work Systems shown as three distinct swim lanes in the cross-functional swim lane diagram shown in Figure 19.1.

1. *Leadership (02)*

2. *Business System Control (BSC)(07)*

3. *Research & Development (R&D)(03)*

INPUT

The primary inputs and triggers of KUP C is *Work System business objectives*. KUP C does not begin until the Work System business objectives are received by Leadership.

Figure 19.1

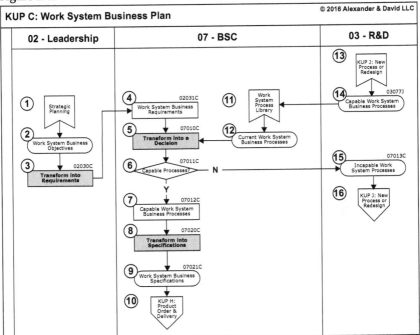

PROCESS

KUP C consists of three Key Work Processes:

02030C
Transform Work System Business Objectives into Work System Business Requirements

Leadership transforms *Work System business objectives* into *Work System business requirements*.

07010C
Transform Work System Business Requirements and Processes into a Decision Identifying Capable Business Processes

BSC transforms the *Work System business requirements* and *Work System business process capabilities* into a *decision* that identifies capable business processes.

07020C
Transform Work System Capable Processes and Business Requirements into Business Specifications

BSC transforms *Work System capable business processes* and *Work System business requirements* into *Work System business specifications*.

OUTPUTS

The throughput output and terminus of KUP C is *Work System business specifications*. Work ends when the *Work System business specifications* are delivered to KUP H. The problem output of KUP C is *incapable Work System business processes*.

STEP-BY-STEP WORK FLOW

KUP C: Work System Business Plan consists of 16 individual steps. The numbers for each step correspond to Figure 19.1.

1. **Strategic Planning**

   Strategic Planning is an upstream process that delivers *Work System business objectives* to KUP C.

2. **Work System Business Objectives**

   Work System business objectives is the throughput output of Strategic Planning.

3. **02030C Transform Work System Business Objectives into Work System Business Requirements**

   Leadership transforms *Work System business objectives* into *Work System business requirements*.

4. **02031C Work System Business Requirements**

   Work System business requirements is the throughput output of Key Work Process 02030C.

5. **07010C Transform Work System Business Requirements and Processes into a Decision Identifying Capable Business Processes**

   BSC transforms the *Work System business*

requirements and *Work System business process capabilities* into a *decision* that identifies capable business processes.

6. 07011C Capable Processes?

BSC decides whether or not current process capabilities can meet the *Work System business requirements*.

7. 07012C Capable Work System Business Processes

Capable Work System business processes is the throughput output of Key Work Process 07010C.

8. 07020C Transform Work System Capable Processes and Business Requirements into Business Specifications

BSC transforms *Work System capable business processes* and *Work System business requirements* into *Work System business specifications*.

9. 07021C Work System Business Specifications

Work System business specifications is the throughput output of Key Work Process 07020C.

10. KUP H: Product Order & Delivery

KUP H is a downstream KUP from Key Work Process 07020C.

11. Work System Process Library

The Work System Process Library contains the existing inventory of *current Work System processes*.

12. Current Work System Business Processes

Current Work System business processes is the throughput output of the Work System Process Library.

13. KUP J: New Process or Redesign

KUP J is an upstream KUP that delivers *capable business processes* to KUP C.

14. 03077J Capable Work System Business Processes

Capable Work System business processes is the throughput output of KUP J.

15. 07013C Incapable Work System Business Processes

Incapable Work System business processes is the problem output of Key Work Process 07010C.

16. KUP J: New Process or Redesign

KUP J is a downstream KUP that receives *incapable Work System processes* from Key Work Process 07010C.

20
KUP D: New Customer Opportunity

DESCRIPTION

KUP D: New Customer Opportunity transforms *Sales business specifications* into a *request for proposal* and *Customer objectives*.

KUP D involves three Key Work Systems (KWS's) shown as three distinct swim lanes in the cross-functional swim lane diagram shown in Figure 20.1:

1. *Sales (04)*
2. *Customer (05)*
3. *CSQA (06)*

INPUT

The primary input and trigger of KUP D is *Sales business specifications*. KUP D does not begin until the *Sales business specifications* are received by Sales.

Figure 20.1

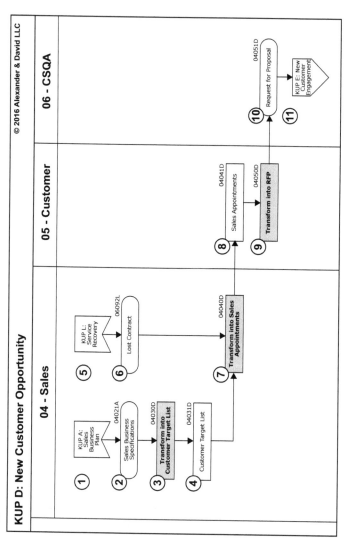

KUP D: New Customer Opportunity

PROCESS

KUP D consists of four Key Work Processes:

04030D
Transform Sales Business Specifications into Customer Target List

Sales transforms *Sales business specifications* into a *Customer target list*.

04040D
Transform Customer Target List into Sales Appointments

Sales transforms the *Customer target list* into *scheduled sales appointments* with prospective Customers.

04050D
Transform Sales Appointments into RFP with Customer Objectives

Sales transforms *introductory sales appointments* into a *request for proposal* with *Customer objectives*.

OUTPUTS

The throughput output and terminus of KUP D is *request for proposal* and *Customer objectives*.

STEP-BY-STEP WORK FLOW

KUP D: New Customer Opportunity consists of 12 individual steps. The numbers for each step correspond to Figure 20.1.

1. KUP A: Sales Business Plan

KUP A is an upstream KUP that delivers *Sales business specifications* to KUP D.

2. 04021A
Sales Business Specifications

Sales business specifications is the throughput output of KUP A.

3. *04030D*
   Transform Sales Business Specifications into Customer Target List

   Sales transforms *Sales business specifications* into a *Customer target list.*

4. *04031D*
   Customer Target List

   Customer target list is the throughput output of KUP A.

5. *KUP L: Service Recovery*

   KUP L is the upstream KUP that delivers a *lost contract* to KUP D.

6. *06092L*
   Lost Contract

   Lost contract is the problem output of KUP L.

7. *04040D*
   Transform Customer Target List into Sales Appointments

   Sales transforms the *Customer target list* into *scheduled sales appointments* with prospective Customers.

8. *04041D*
   Sales Appointments

   Sales Appointments are the throughput outputs of Key Work Process 04040D.

9. *04050D*
   Transform Sales Appointments into RFP with Customer Objectives

   Sales transforms *introductory sales appointments* into a *request for proposal* with *Customer objectives.*

10. *04051D*
    Request for Proposal with Customer Objectives

    The *request for proposal with Customer objectives* is the throughout output of Key Work Process 04050D.

11. KUP E: New Customer Engagement

KUP E is the downstream KUP that receives the *request for proposal with Customer objectives* from KUP D.

21
KUP E: New Customer Engagement

Description

KUP E: New Customer Engagement transforms *a request for proposal with Customer objectives* into an *accepted contract.*

KUP E involves three Key Work Systems (KWS's) shown as three distinct swim lanes in the cross-functional swim lane diagram (Figure 21.1):

1. *CSQA (06)*
2. *R&D (03)*
3. *Customer (05)*

INPUT

The primary inputs and triggers of KUP E are *request for proposal with Customer objectives.* KUP E does not begin until the re*quest for proposal with Customer objectives* are received by CSQA.

Figure 21.1

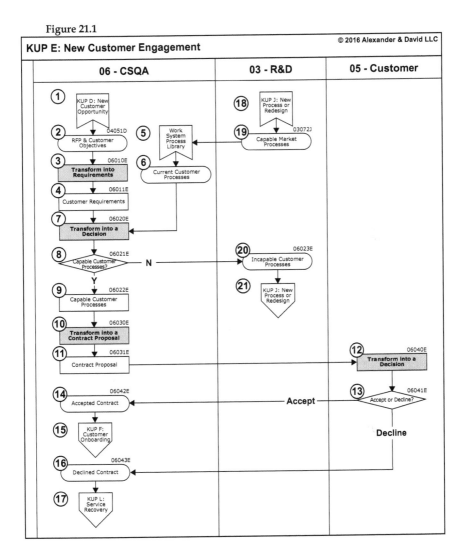

PROCESS

KUP E consists of four Key Work Processes:

06010E
Transform Customer Objectives into Customer Requirements

CSQA transforms *Customer objectives* into *Customer requirements.*

06020E
Transform Customer Requirements and Processes into a Decision Identifying Capable Processes

CSQA transforms *Customer requirements* and *current Customer process capabilities* into a *decision* that identifies capable processes.

06030E
Transform Capable Processes with Customer Requirements into a Contract Proposal

CSQA transforms *capable processes with Customer requirements* into a *contract proposal*.

06040E
Transform Contract Proposal into a Customer Decision to Accept or Decline

CSQA transforms *contract proposal* into a *Customer decision* to accept or decline.

OUTPUTS

The throughput output and terminus of KUP E is an *accepted contract*. Work ends when the *accepted contract* is delivered to downstream KUP F: Customer On-boarding. The problem outputs for KUP E are *incapable Customer processes* and *declined contract*.

STEP-BY-STEP WORK FLOW

KUP E: New Customer Engagement consists of 23 individual steps. The numbers for each step correspond to Figure 21.1.

1. **KUP D: New Customer Opportunity**

   KUP D is an upstream KUP that delivers a *request for proposal with Customer objectives* to KUP E.

2. **04051D**
   Request for Proposal with Customer Objectives

   The *request for proposal with Customer objectives* is the throughput output of KUP D.

3. **06010E**
   Transform Customer Objectives into Customer Requirements

   CSQA transforms *Customer objectives* into *Customer requirements*.

4. **06011E**
   Customer Requirements

   Customer requirements is the throughput output of Key Work Process 06010E.

5. **Work System Process Library**

   The Work System Process Library contains the existing inventory of *current Customer processes*.

6. **Current Customer Processes**

   Current Customer processes is the throughput output of the Work System Process Library.

7. **06020E**
   Transform Customer Requirements and Processes into a Decision Identifying Capable Processes

   CSQA transforms *Customer requirements* and *current Customer process capabilities* into a *decision* that identifies capable processes.

8. **06021E Capable Processes?**

   CSQA decides whether or not *current process capabilities* can meet the *Customer requirements*.

9. **06022E**
   Capable Customer Processes and Customer Requirements

   Capable Customer processes and requirements is the throughput output of Key Work Process 06020E.

10. **06030E**
    Transform Capable Processes with Customer Requirements into a Contract Proposal

    CSQA transforms *capable processes with Customer*

requirements into a *contract proposal.*

11. 06031E
Contract Proposal

The *contract proposal* is the throughput output of Key Work Process 06030E.

12. 06040E
Transform Contract Proposal into a Customer Decision to Accept or Decline

CSQA transforms *contract proposal* into a *Customer decision* to accept or decline.

13. 06041E
Accept/Decline?

Customer *decides* whether to *accept or decline* the contract proposal.

14. 06042E
Accepted Contract

The *accepted contract* is the throughput output of Key Work Process 06040E.

15. KUP F: Customer On-boarding

KUP F is the downstream KUP that receives the *accepted contract* from KUP E.

16. 06043E
Declined Contract

The *declined contract* is the problem output of KUP E. and receives the problem output

17. KUP L: Service Recovery

KUP L is the downstream KUP that receives the *declined contract* problem output from Key Work Process 06040E.

18. KUP J: New Process or Redesign

KUP J is the upstream KUP that delivers *capable market processes* to KUP E.

19. *03072J*

Capable Market Processes

Capable market processes is the throughput output of KUP J.

20. *06023E*

Incapable Customer Processes

Incapable Customer processes is the problem output of Key Work Process 06020E.

21. KUP J: New Process or Redesign

KUP J is the downstream KUP that receives the *incapable Customer processes* problem output from Key Work Process 06020E.

22
KUP F: Customer On-Boarding

DESCRIPTION

KUP F: Customer On-Boarding transforms an *accepted contract* from a new Customer or an *accepted modified contract* from a current Customer into an *approved Communications and Conflict Resolution Plan (CCRP)* and a list of *multiple qualified Suppliers*.

KUP F involves three Key Work Systems (KWS's) shown as three distinct swim lanes in the cross-functional swim lane diagram in Figure 21.1:

1. *Customer (05)*

2. *CSQA (06)*

3. *R&D (03)*

INPUT

The primary inputs and triggers of KUP F are an accepted contract or an accepted modified contract. KUP F does not begin until an

Figure 22.1

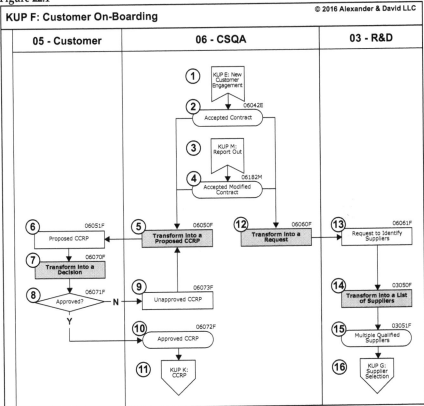

accepted contract or accepted modified contract is received by CSQA.

PROCESS

KUP F consists of four Key Work Processes:

06050F
Transform Accepted Contract or Unapproved CCRP into a Proposed CCRP

CSQA transforms an *accepted contract* into a *proposed Communication and Conflict Resolution Plan (CCRP).*

06060F
Transform Accepted Contract into a Request to Identify Qualified Suppliers

CSQA transforms the *accepted contract* into a *request to identify multiple qualified suppliers.*

06070F
Transform Proposed CCRP into a Customer Decision to Approve or Decline

CSQA transforms the *proposed Communication and Conflict Resolution Plan (CCRP)* into a *Customer decision* to approve or decline the CCRP.

03050F
Transform Request into Multiple Qualified Suppliers

R&D transforms the *request to identify multiple qualified Suppliers* into a *list of multiple qualified Suppliers.*

OUTPUTS

The throughput output and terminus of KUP F is an *approved CCRP* and *multiple qualified Suppliers*. Work ends when the approved CCRP is delivered to downstream KUP K: CCRP and when the multiple qualified Suppliers is delivered to downsteam KUP G: Supplier Selection.

STEP-BY-STEP WORK FLOW

KUP F: Customer On-Boarding consists of 16 individual steps. The numbers each step correspond to Figure 22.1.

1. ### *KUP E: New Customer Enagement*

    KUP E: New Customer Engagement is the upstream KUP that delivers an *accepted contract* to Key Work Processes 06050F and 06060F.

2. ### *06042E*
    ### *Accepted Contract*

    The *accepted contract* is the throughput output of KUP E.

3. **KUP M: Report Out**

    KUP M: Report Out is the upstream KUP that delivers an *accepted modified contract* to Key Work Processes 06050F and 06060F.

4. **06082M**
    Accepted Modified Contract

    The *accepted modified contract* is the throughput output of KUP M.

5. **06050F**
    Transform Accepted Contract into a Proposed CCRP

    CSQA transforms an *accepted contract* into a *proposed Communication and Conflict Resolution Plan (CCRP)*.

6. **06051F**
    Proposed CCRP

    The *proposed CCRP* is the throughput output of Key Work Process 06050F.

7. **06070F**
    Transform Proposed CCRP into a Customer Decision to Approve or Decline

    CSQA transforms the *proposed Communication and Conflict Resolution Plan (CCRP)* into a *Customer decision* to approve or decline the CCRP.

8. **06071F Approved?**

    The Customer decides whether or not to accept or decline the CCRP.

9. **06073F**
    Unapproved CCRP

    An *unapproved CCRP* is the problem output of Key Work Process 06070F.

10. **06072F**
    Approved CCRP

    An *approved CCRP* is the throughput output of Key Work Process 06070F.

11. KUP K: CCRP

KUP K: CCRP is the downstream KUP that receives an *approved CCRP* from KUP F.

12. 06060F

Transform Accepted Contract into a Request to Identify Multiple Suppliers

CSQA transforms the *accepted contract* into a *request to identify multiple qualified suppliers.*

13. 06061F

Request to Identify Multiple Suppliers

The *request to identify multiple Supplier* is the throughput output of Key Work Process 06060M.

14. 03050F

Transform Request to Identify Suppliers into Multiple Qualified Suppliers

R&D transforms the *request to identify multiple qualified Suppliers* into a *list of multiple qualified Suppliers.*

15. 03051F

Multiple Qualified Suppliers

The *list of multiple qualified Suppliers* is the throughput output of Key Work Process 03050F.

16. KUP G: Supplier Selection

KUP G: Supplier Selection is the downstream KUP that receives the *list of multiple qualified Suppliers* from KUP F.

23
KUP G: Supplier Selection

DESCRIPTION

KUP G: Supplier Selection transforms the *list of multiple qualified Suppliers* and *Customer order specifications* into *resources, materials, or parts* delivered to KUP H: Product Order & Delivery.

1. *BSC (07)*
2. *Supplier (08)*
3. *Production System (09)*

INPUT

The primary inputs and triggers of KUP G are the *list of multiple qualified Suppliers* and the *Customer order specifications*. KUP G does not begin until both the *list of multiple qualified Suppliers* and *Customer order specifications* are received by BSC.

PROCESS

KUP G consists of seven Key Work Processes:

Figure 23.1

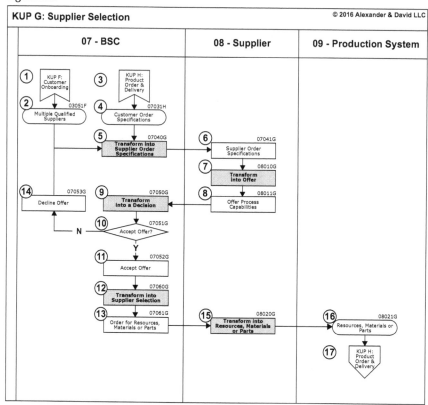

07040G
Transform Customer Order Specifications, Multiple Qualified Suppliers and Decline Offer into Supplier Order Specifications

BSC transforms the *Customer order specifications, the list of multiple qualified Suppliers* and a *declined offer* into Supplier order specifications.

08010G
Transform Supplier Order Specifications into an Offer of Process Capabilities

The Supplier transforms the *Supplier order specifications* into an *offer of process capabilities*.

07050G
Transform Supplier Offer Process Capabilities into a Decision to Accept or Decline
BSC transforms the *Supplier offer of process capabilities* into a *decision* whether or not to accept or decline the offer.

07060G
Transform Accepted Offer into Order for Resources, Materials or Parts
BSC transforms the *accepted offer* into an *order* for resources, materials or parts.

08020G
Transform Order into Resources, Materials or Parts
The Supplier transforms an *order* for resources, materials or parts into the *resources, materials or parts*.

OUTPUTS

The throughput output and terminus of KUP G are the *resources, materials or parts*. Work ends when the *resources, materials or parts* are delivered to downstream KUP H: Product Order & Delivery.

STEP-BY-STEP WORK FLOW

KUP G: Supplier Selection consists of 23 individual steps. The numbers each step correspond to Figure 23.1.

1. *KUP F: Customer On-Boarding*
KUP F is the upstream KUP that delivers the *list of multiple qualified Suppliers* to KUP G.

2. *03051F*
Multiple Qualified Suppliers
The list of multiple qualified Suppliers is the throughput output of KUP F.

3. *KUP H: Product Order & Delivery*
KUP H is the upstream KUP that delivers the *Customer order specifications* to KUP G.

4. *07031H*

    Customer Order Specifications for Supplier

    The *Customer order specifications* is the throughput output of KUP H.

5. *07040G*

    Transform Customer Order Specifications, Multiple Qualified Suppliers and Decline Offer into Supplier Order Specifications

    BSC transforms the *Customer order specifications, the list of multiple qualified Suppliers* and a *declined offer* into Supplier order specifications.

6. *07041G*

    Supplier Order Specifications

    The *Supplier order specifications* is the throughput output of Key Work Process 07040G.

7. *08010G*

    Transform Supplier Order Specifications into an Offer of Process Capabilities

    The Supplier transforms the *Supplier order specifications* into an *offer of process capabilities.*

8. *08011G Offer of Process Capabilities*

    The *offer of process capabilities* is the throughput output of Key Work Process 08010G.
    08030G.

9. *07050G*

    Transform Supplier Offer Process Capabilities into a Decision to Accept or Decline

    BSC transforms the *Supplier offer of process capabilities* into a *decision* whether or not to accept or decline the offer.

10. *07051G Accept or Decline?*

    BSC decides whether or not to accept or decline the *offer of process capabilities.*

11. 07052G
Accept Offer
The *accept offer* is the throughput output of Key Work Process 07050G.

12. 07052G
Decline Offer
The *decline offer* is the problem output of Key Work Process 07050G.

13. 08020G
Transform Order into Resources, Materials or Parts
The Supplier transforms an *order* for resources, materials or parts into the *resources, materials or parts*.

14. 08021G
Resources, Materials or Parts
The *resources, materials or parts* is the throughput output of Key Work Process 08020G.

15. KUP H: Product Order & Delivery
KUP H is the downstream KUP that receives *the resources, materials or parts* from KUP G.

24
KUP H: Product Order & Delivery

DESCRIPTION

KUP H: Product Order & Delivery transforms *Customer order objectives* into *finished products or services* delivered to the Consumer.

KUP H involves six Key Work Systems (KWS's) shown as six distinct swim lanes in the cross-functional KUP diagram shown in Figure 24.1:

1. *R&D (03)*
2. *CSQA (06)*
3. *BSC (07)*
4. *Supplier (08)*
5. *Production System (09)*
6. *Consumer (10)*

Figure 24.1

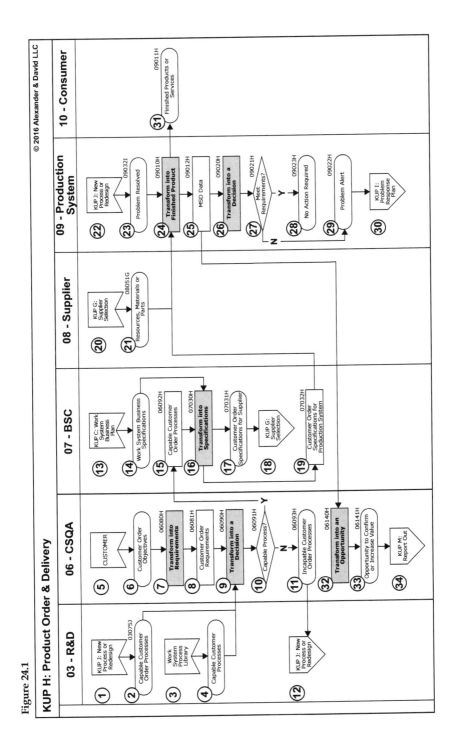

KUP H: Product Order & Delivery

© 2016 Alexander & David LLC

INPUT

The primary input and trigger of KUP H are the *Customer order objectives*. KUP H does not begin until the Customer order objectives are received by CSQA.

PROCESS

KUP H consists of six Key Work Processes:

06080H
Transform Customer Order Objectives into Customer Order Requirements

CSQA transforms *Customer order objectives* into *Customer order requirements*.

06090H
Transform Customer Order Requirements and Process Capabilities into a Decision Identifying Capable Processes

CSQA transforms *Customer order requirements* and *Customer process capabilities* into a *decision* that identifies capable processes.

07030H
Transform Customer Order Requirements and Capable Customer Order Processes into Customer Order Specifications

BSC transforms the *Customer order requirements* and *capable Customer order processes* into *Customer order specifications*.

09010H
Transform Customer Order Specifications; Resources, Materials or Parts; and Problems Resolved into Finished Products or Services

The Production System transforms *Customer order specifications; resurces, materials, or parts*; and *problems resolved* into finished product or services.

09020H

Transform MSD Data into a Decision whether or not to issue a Problem Alert

> The Production System transforms the *Measurement System Design data* into a *decision* whether or not to issue a problem alert.

06140H

Transform MSD Data into Opportunity to Confirm or Increase Value

> CSQA transforms *Measurement System Design data* into an *opportunity to confirm or increase value.*

OUTPUTS

The throughput output and terminus of KUP H is the *finished product or service.* Work ends when the finished product or service is delivered to the Consumer. The problem outputs of KUP H are *incapable Customer order processes,* and *problem alerts.*

STEP-BY-STEP WORK FLOW

KUP H: Product Order & Delivery consists of 35 individual steps. (Numbers correspond to Figure 24.1.)

1. **KUP J: New Process or Design**

   > KUP J is an upstream KUP that delivers *Capable Customer order processes* to KUP H.

2. **03075J**

   Capable Customer Order Processes

   > *Capable Customer order processes* is the throughput output of KUP J.

3. **Work System Process Library**

   > The Work System Process Library contains the existing inventory of *current Work System processes.*

4. Capable Customer Processes

Capable Customer processes processes is the throughput output of the Work System Process Library.

5. Customer

Currently engaged Customers.

6. Customer Order Objectives

Capable order objectives is the throughput output of the Customer.

7. 06080H

Transform Customer Order Objectives into Customer Order Requirements

CSQA transforms *Customer order objectives* into *Customer order requirements*.

8. 06081H

Customer Order Requirements

Capable order requirements is the throughput output of Key Work Process 06080H.

9. 06090H

Transform Customer Order Requirements and Process Capabilities into a Decision Identifying Capable Processes

CSQA transforms *Customer order requirements* and *Customer process capabilities* into a *decision* that identifies capable processes.

10. 06091H Capable Processes?

CSQA decides whether or not current process capabilities can meet the *Customer order requirements*.

11. 06093H

Incapable Customer Order Processes

Incapable Customer order processes is the throughput output of Key Work Process 06090H.

12. KUP J: New Process or Design

KUP J is a downstream KUP that receives *incapable Customer order processes* from Key Work Process 06090H.

13. KUP C: Work System Business Plan

KUP J is an upstream KUP that delivers *Work System business specifications* to KUP H.

14. 07021H
Work System Business Specifications

Work System business specifications is the throughput output of KUP C.

15. 06092H
Capable Customer Order Processes and Customer Order Requirements

Capable Customer order processes and *Customer order requirements* are the throughput outputs of Key Work Process 06090H.

16. 07030H
Transform Customer Order Requirements and Capable Customer Order Processes into Customer Order Specifications

BSC transforms the *Customer order requirements* and *capable Customer order processes* into *Customer order specifications*.

17. 07031H
Customer Order Specifications for Supplier

Customer order specifications for Supplier is the throughput output of Key Work Process 07030H.

18. KUP G: Supplier Selection

KUP G is a downstream KUP that receives *Customer order specifications for Supplier* from KUP H.

19. 07032H

Customer Order Specifications for Production System

Customer order specifications for Production System and capable Customer order processes are the throughput outputs of Key Work Process 07030H.

20. KUP G: Supplier Selection

KUP G is an upstream KUP that delivers resources, materials or parts to KUP H.

21. 08051G

Resources, Materials, or Parts

Resources, materials or parts is the throughput output of KUP G.

22. KUP J: New Process or Redesign

KUP J is an upstream KUP that delivers a problem resolved to KUP H.

23. 09032H

Problem Resolved

Problem resolved is the throughput output of Key KUP J.

24. 09010H

Transform Customer Order Specifications; Resources, Materials or Parts; and Problems Resolved into Finished Products or Services

The Production System transforms Customer order specifications; resurces, materials, or parts; and problems resolved into finished product or services.

25. 09012H

Measurement System Design Data

Measurement system design data is the throughput output of Key Work Process 09010H.

26. 09020H
Transform MSD Data into a Decision whether or not to issue a Problem Alert

The Production System transforms the *Measurement System Design data* into a *decision* whether or not to issue a problem alert.

27. 09021H Meet Requirements?

The Production System decides whether or not to issue a *problem alert*.

28. 09024H
No Action Required

No action required is the throughput output of Key Work Process 09020H.

29. 09022H
Problem Alert

Problem alert is the problem output of Key Work Process 09020H.

30. KUP I: Problem Response Plan

KUP J is a downstream KUP that receives *problem alert* from KUP H.

31. 09011H
Finished Products or Services

Finished products or services in the throughput output and terminus of KUP H.

32. 06040E
Transform MSD Data into Opportunity to Confirm or Increase Value

CSQA transforms *Measurement System Design data* into an *opportunity to confirm or increase value*.

33. 06141H
Opportunity to Confirm or Increase Value

The *opportunity to confirm or increase value* is the throughput output of Key Work Process 06040E.

34. KUP M: Report Out

KUP M is a downstream KUP that receives the *opportunity to confirm or increase value incapable* from KUP H.

25
KUP I: Problem Response Plan

DESCRIPTION

KUP I: Problem Response Plan transforms a *problem alert* into a *problem resolved* and a *decision* whether or not to activate the Communcations and Conflict Resolution Plan (CCRP).

KUP I involves three Key Work Systems (KWS's) shown as three distinct swim lanes in the cross-functional KUP diagram shown in Figure 25.1:

1. *Production System (09)*

2. *R&D (03)*

3. *CSQA (06)*

INPUT

The primary input and trigger of KUP I is a *problem alert*. KUP I does not begin until the problem alert is received.

PROCESS

KUP E consists of two Key Work Processes:

09030I
Transform Problem Alert into a Decision whether or not Problem is Resolved

The Production System transforms a *problem alert* into a *decision* whether or not the problem is resolved.

06100I
Transform Problem Alert into Decision to Activate CCRP

CSQA transforms the *problem alert* into a *decision* whether or not to activate Communications and Conflict Resolution Plan (CCRP).

OUTPUTS

The throughput output and terminus of KUP I is a *problem resolved*. Work ends when the problem resolved is delivered to downstream KUP H: Product Order & Delivery. The problem outputs of KUP I are *problems unresolved* and *CCRP activated*.

STEP-BY-STEP WORK FLOW

KUP I: Problem Response consists of 15 individual steps. The numbers for each step correspond to Figure 25.1.

1. **KUP H: Product Order & Delivery**

    KUP H is an upstream KUP that delivers a *problem alert* to KUP I.

2. **09022H**
    Problem Alert

    The *problem alert* is a problem output of KUP H.

3. **09030I**
    Transform Problem Alert into a Decision Whether Problem is Resolved

    The Production System transforms a *problem alert* into a *decision* whether or not the problem is resolved.

Figure 25.1

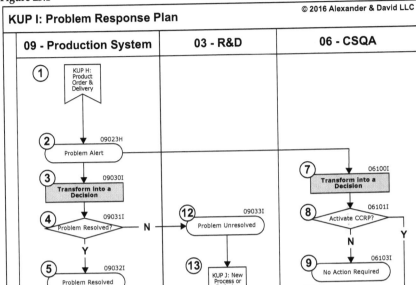

4. 09031I Problem Resolved?

The Production System decides whether or not the *problem is resolved.*

5. 09032I
Problem Resolved

The *problem resolved* is a throughput output of Key Work Process 9030I.

6. KUP H: Product Order & Delivery

KUP H is the downstream KUP that receives the *problem resolved* from KUP I.

7. **061000I**

   Transform Problem Alert into Decision to Activate CCRP

   CSQA transforms the *problem alert* into a *decision* whether or not to activate Communications and Conflict Resolution Plan (CCRP).

8. **06101I Activate CCRP?**

   The CSQA decides whether or not the to activate the *Communication and Conflict Resolution Plan (CCRP)*.

9. **06103I**

   No Action Required

   No action required is the throughput output of Key Work Process 06100I.

10. **06102I**

    CCRP Activated

    CCRP activated is the problem output of Key Work Process 06100I.

11. **KUP K: CCRP**

    KUP K is the downstream KUP that receives the *CCRP activated* from KUP I.

12. **09032I**

    Problem Unresolved

    The *problem unresolved* is the problem output of Key Work Process 09030I.

13. **KUP J: New Process or Redesign**

    KUP J is the downstream KUP that receives the *problem unresolved* from KUP I.

26
KUP J: New Process or Redesign

KUP DESCRIPTION

KUP J: New Process or Redesign transforms *incapable processes* from multiple Key Work Systems into *proposals to build or redesign*. KUP J then transforms a *decision to build* from Leadership into *capable processes*. KUP J also transforms *problems unresolved* from the Production System into *problems resolved*.

KUP J involves six Key Work Systems shown as six distinct swim lanes in the cross-functional swim lane diagram shown in Figure 26.1:

1. *Leadership (02)*

2. *R&D (03)*

3. *Sales (04)*

4. *CSQA (06)*

5. *BSC (07)*

6. *Production System (09)*

INPUT TO KUP

The primary inputs and triggers of KUP J are *incapable processes* and *problems unresolved*. KUP J does not begin until the incapable processes or problem unresolved are received by R&D.

KUP PROCESS

KUP J consists of four Key Work Processes:

03060J
Transform Incapable Processes into a Proposal to Build or Redesign

R&D transforms *incapable processes* or *problems unresolved* into a *proposal to build or redesign*.

02040J
Transform Proposal into a Decision to Accept or Request Additional Information

Leadership transforms the *proposal to build or redesign* into a *decision to accept or request additional information*.[26.2]

02050J
Transform Accepted Proposal into a Decision to Build or Pass

Leadership transforms an *accepted proposal* into a *decision to build or pass*.

03070J
Transform a Decision to Build into a Capable Process

R&D transforms the *decision to build* into a *capable process* or a *problem resolved*.

OUTPUTS

The throughput outputs and terminus of KUP J are *capable processes* or *problems resolved*. Work ends when these outputs are delivered.

STEP-BY-STEP WORK FLOW

KUP J: New Process or Redesign consists of 45 individual steps. The numbers for each step correspond to Figure 26.1.

1. KUP B: R&D Business Plan

KUP B is an upstream KUP that delivers *incapable business processes* and *incapable market processes* to KUP J.

2. 03013B
Incapable R&D Business Processes

Incapable R&D business processes are problem outputs of KUP B.

3. 03043B
Incapable Market Processes

Incapable Market processes are problem outputs of KUP B.

4. R&D Process Library

The *R&D Process Library* contains the existing inventory of stable, repeatable and reproducible R&D business processes.

5. 03043B
Capable R&D Processes

Capable R&D business processes are throughput outputs of the R&D Tool Box.

6. KUP A: Sales Business Plan

KUP A is an upstream KUP that delivers *incapable Sales business processes* to KUP J.

7. 04013A
Incapable Sales Business Processes

Incapable Sales business processes are problem outputs of KUP A.

8. KUP E: New Customer Engagement

KUP E is an upstream KUP that delivers *incapable*

Figure 26.1

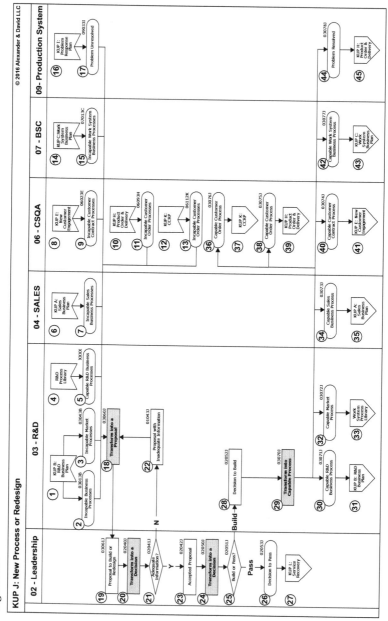

Customer contract processes to KUP J.

9. *06023E*
Incapable Customer Contract Processes

Incapable Customer contract processes are problem outputs of KUP E.

10. KUP H: Product Order & Delivery

KUP H is an upstream KUP that delivers *incapable Customer order processes* to KUP J.

11. *06093H*
Incapable Customer Order Processes

Incapable Customer order processes are problem outputs of KUP E.

12. KUP K: CCRP

KUP K is an upstream KUP that delivers *incapable Customer order processes* to KUP J.

13. *06112K*
Incapable Customer Order Processes

Incapable Customer order processes are problem outputs of KUP K.

14. KUP C: Work System Business Plan

KUP C is an upstream KUP that delivers *incapable Work System business processes* to KUP J.

15. *06112K*
Incapable Work System Business Processes

Incapable Work System business processes are problem outputs of KUP C.

16. KUP I: Problem Response Plan

KUP I is an upstream KUP that delivers *problem unresolved* to KUP J.

17. *09033IK*
Problem Unresolved

Problem unresolved is a problem output of KUP C.

18. 03060J
Transform Incapable Processes into a Proposal to Build or Redesign

R&D transforms *incapable processes* or *problems unresolved* into a *proposal to build or redesign.*

19. 03061J
Proposal to Build or Redesign

A *proposal to build or redesign* is a throughput output of KWP 03060J.

20. 02040J
Transform Proposal to Build or Redesign into a Decision to Accept or Request Additional Information

Leadership transforms the *proposal to build or redesign* into a *decision to accept or request additional information.*

21. 02040J
Adequate Information?

Leadership *decides* whether or not the proposal to build or redesign has adequate information.[26.1]

22. 01043J
Proposal with Inadequate Information

Proposal with inadequate information is a problem output of KWP 02040J.

23. 02042J
Accepted Proposal

Accepted proposal is a throughput output of KWP 02040J.

24. 02050J
Transform Accepted Proposal into a Decision to Build or Pass

Leadership transforms an *accepted proposal* into a *decision to build or pass.*

25. 02050J
Build or Pass?
Leadership *decides* whether or not to build or pass.

26. 02053J
Decision to Pass
Decision to pass is a problem output of KWP 02050J.

27. KUP L: Service Recovery
KUP L is a downstream KUP that receives the *decision to pass* from KWP 02050J.

28. 02052J
Decision to Build
Decision to build is a throughput output of KWP 02050J.

29. 03070J
Transform a Decision to Build into a Capable Process
R&D transforms the *decision to build* into a *capable process* or a *problem resolved.*

30. 03071J
Capable R&D Business Processes
Capable R&D business processes are throughput outputs of KWP 03070J.

31. KUP B: R&D Business Plan
KUP B is a downstream KUP that receives the *capable R&D business processes* from KWP 03070J.

32. 03072J
Capable Market Processes
Capable Market processes are throughput outputs of KWP 03070J.

33. Work System Process Library
KUP E is a downstream KUP that receives the *capable Market processes* from KWP 03070J.

The Work System Process Library contains the existing inventory of *current Work System processes*.

34. 03073J
Capable Sales Business Processes

Capable Sales business processes are throughput outputs of KWP 03070J.

35. KUP A: Sales Business Plan

KUP A is a downstream KUP that receives the *capable Sales business processes* from KWP 03070J.

36. 03076J
Capable Customer Order Processes

Capable Customer order processes are throughput outputs of KWP 03070J.

37. KUP K: CCRP

KUP K is a downstream KUP that receives the *capable Customer order processes* from KWP 03070J.

38. 03075J
Capable Customer Order Processes

Capable Customer order processes are throughput outputs of KWP 03070J.

39. KUP H: Product Order and Delivery

KUP H is a downstream KUP that receives the *capable Customer order processes* from KWP 03070J.

40. 03074J
Capable Customer Contract Processes

Capable Customer contract processes are throughput outputs of KWP 03070J.

41. KUP E: New Customer Engagement

KUP E is a downstream KUP that receives the *capable Customer contract processes* from KWP 03070J.

42. 03077J

Capable Work System Business Processes

Capable Work System business processes are throughput outputs of KWP 03070J.

43. KUP C: Work System Business Plan

KUP C is a downstream KUP that receives the *capable Work System business processes* from KWP 03070J.

44. 03078J

Problem Resolved

Problem resolved is a throughput output of KWP 03070J.

45. KUP I: Problem Response Plan

KUP H is a downstream KUP that receives the *problem resolved* from KWP 03070J.

27
KUP K: CCRP

DESCRIPTION

KUP K: Communication and Conflict Resolution Plan (CCRP) transforms a *CCRP activated* into an *issue resolved*.

KUP K involves three Key Work Systems shown as three distinct swim lanes in the cross-functional swim-lane diagram shown in Figure 27.1:

1. *Customer (05)*

2. *CSQA (06)*

3. *R&D (03)*

INPUT

The primary input and trigger of KUP K is a *CCRP activated*. A secondary input is *approved CCRP*. KUP K does not begin until both the *CCRP activated* and *approved CCRP* are received by the CSQA KWS.

Figure 27.1

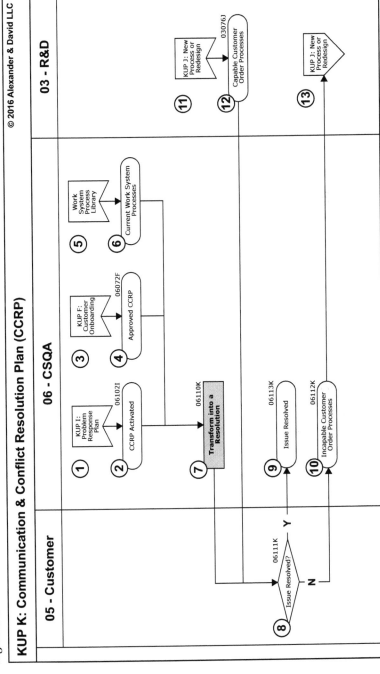

KUP K: Communication & Conflict Resolution Plan (CCRP)

© 2016 Alexander & David LLC

PROCESS

KUP K consists of one Key Work Process:

06110K
Transform Activated CCRP into a Resolution

CSQA receives *approved CCRP* and *CCRP activated* and transforms them into a *decision* whether or not the issue is resolved.

OUTPUTS

The throughput output and terminus of KUP K is an *issue resolved*. Work ends when the *issue resolved* is delivered to CSQA.

A problem output of KUP K is *incapable Customer order processes*.

STEP-BY-STEP WORK FLOW

KUP K: CCRP consists of 11 individual steps. The numbers for each step correspond to Figure 27.1.

1. **KUP F: Customer Onboarding**
    KUP D is an upstream KUP that delivers *approved CCRP* to KUP K.

2. **06072F**
    Approved CCRP
    An *approved CCRP* is a throughput output of KUP F.

3. **KUP I: Problem Response Plan**
    KUP I is an upstream KUP that delivers *CCRP activated* to KUP K.

4. **06102I**
    CCRP Activated
    CCRP activated is a problem output of KUP C.

5. **06110K**
    Transform Activated CCRP into a Resolution
    CSQA receives *approved CCRP* and *CCRP activated* and

transforms them into a *decision* whether or not the issue is resolved.

6. 06111K Issue Resolved?

CSQA and Customer decide whether or not the CCRP has produced an *issue resolved*.

7. 06113K
Issue Resolved

Issue resolved is a throughput output of KWP 06110K.

8. 06112K
Incapable Customer Order Processes

Incapable Customer order processes is a problem output of KWP 06110K.

9. KUP J: New Process or Design

KUP J is a downstream KUP that receives the *incapable Customer order processes* from KWP 06110K.

10. KUP J: New Process or Design

KUP J is an upstream KUP that delivers *capable Customer order processes* to KUP K.

11. 03076J
Capable Customer Order Processes

Capable Customer order processes is a throughput output of KUP J.

28
KUP L: Service Recovery

DESCRIPTION

KUP L: Service Recovery transforms a *declined contract* or *decision to pass* into an *accepted solution*.

KUP L involves five Key Work Systems shown as five distinct swim lanes in the cross-functional swim lane diagram shown in Figure 28.1:

1. *Customer (05)*

2. *CSQA (06)*

3. *R&D (03)*

4. *Sales (04)*

5. *Leadership (02)*

INPUT

The primary inputs and triggers of KUP L are *declined contract* and *decision to pass*. KUP L does not begin until either a *declined contract* or a *decision to pass* is received.

PROCESS

KUP L consists of three Key Work Processes:

03080L
Transform a Declined Contract into an Identified External Solution

R&D transforms a *declined contract* or a *decision to pass* into a *decision* identifying an external solution.

06120L
Transform Identified External Solution into Customer Decision to Accept or Decline

CSQA transforms *identified external solution* into a Customer *decision* to accept or decline.

06130L
Transform Accepted Solution into a Retained or Lost Contract

CSQA transforms *accepted solution* into a *retained or lost contract.*

OUTPUTS

The throughput output and terminus of KUP L is either *retained contract* or *lost contract.* Work ends when a *retained contract* is secured or a *lost contract* is delivered to KUP D.

STEP-BY-STEP WORK FLOW

KUP L: Service Recovery consists of 17 individual steps. The numbers for each step correspond to Figure 28.1.

1. KUP E: New Customer Engagement

KUP E is an upstream KUP that delivers a *declined contract* to KUP L.

2. 06043E
Decline Contract

Declined contract is a problem output of KUP E.

Figure 28.1

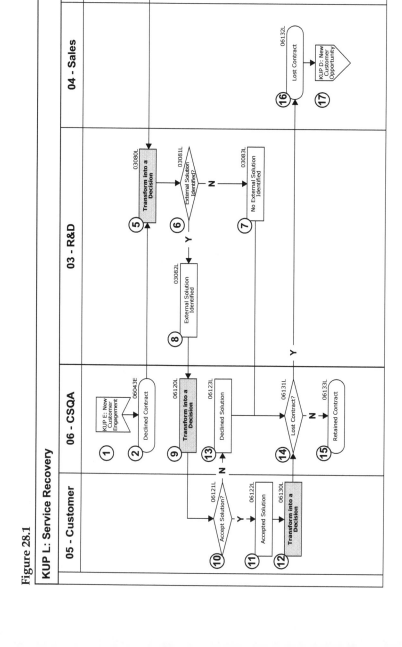

3. **KUP J: New Process or Redesign**

   KUP J is an upstream KUP that delivers a *decision to pass* to KUP L.

4. **02053J**
   Decision to Pass

   Decision to Pass is a problem output of KUP J.

5. **03080L**
   Transform a Declined Contract into an Identified External Solution

   R&D transforms a *declined contract* or a *decision to pass* into a *decision* identifying an external solution.

6. **03081L External Solution Identified?**

   R&D decides whether or not an *external solution has been identified.*

7. **03083L**
   No External Solution Identified

   No external solution identified is a problem output of KWP 03080L.

8. **03082L**
   External Solution Identified

   External solution identified is a throughput output of KWP 03080L.

9. **06120L**
   Transform Identified External Solution into Customer Decision to Accept or Decline

   CSQA transforms *identified external solution* into a Customer *decision* to accept or decline.

10. **06121L Accept?**

    Customer decides whether or not to *accept or decline* the identified external solution.

11. *06130L*
Accepted Solution
Accepted solution is a throughput output of KWP 06120L.

12. *06130L*
Transform Accepted Solution into a Decision
CSQA transforms *accepted solution* into a *decision* whether contract is retained or lost.

13. *06123L*
Declined Solution
A *declined solution* is a problem output of KWP 06120L.

14. *06131L Lost Contract?*
CSQA decides whether contract has been *retained* or *lost*.

15. *06133L*
Retained Contract
Retained contract is a throughput output of KWP 06130L.

16. *06132L*
Lost Contract
Lost contract is a problem output of KWP 06130L.

17. *KUP D: New Customer Opportunity*
KUP D is a downstream KUP that receives the *lost contract* from KUP L.

29
KUP M: Report Out

DESCRIPTION

KUP M: Report Out transforms an *opportunity to confirm or increase value* into an *accepted modified contract.*

KUP M involves two Key Work Systems shown as two distinct swim lanes in the cross-functional KUP diagrams shown in Figure 29.1:

1. *CSQA (06)*
2. *Customer (05)*

INPUT

The primary input and trigger of KUP M is *opportunity to confirm or increase value*. KUP M does not begin until the *opportunity to confirm or increase value* are received by CSQA.

PROCESS

KUP M consists of four Key Work Processes:

1. **06150M**
   Transform Opportunity to Confirm or Increase Value into Report
   CSQA transforms *an opportunity to confirm or increase value* into a *report*.

2. **06160M**
   Transform Report into Decision to Approve Value Increase
   CSQA transforms the *report* into a *decision* to approve value increase.

3. **06170M**
   Transform Current Contract into Proposed Modified Contract
   CSQA transforms an *approved value increase* into a *proposed modified contract*.

4. **06180M**
   Transform Proposed Modified Contract into Decision to Accept Contract
   CSQA transforms a *proposed modified contract* into a *decision* to accept contract.

OUTPUTS

The throughput output and terminus of KUP M is an *accepted modified contract*. Work ends when the *accepted modified contract* is delivered to KUP F.

STEP-BY-STEP WORK FLOW

KUP M: Report Out consists of 15 individual steps. The numbers for each step correspond to Figure 29.1.

1. **KUP H: Product Order & Delivery**
   KUP H is an upstream KUP that delivers an *opportunity to confirm or increase value* to KUP M.

Figure 29.1

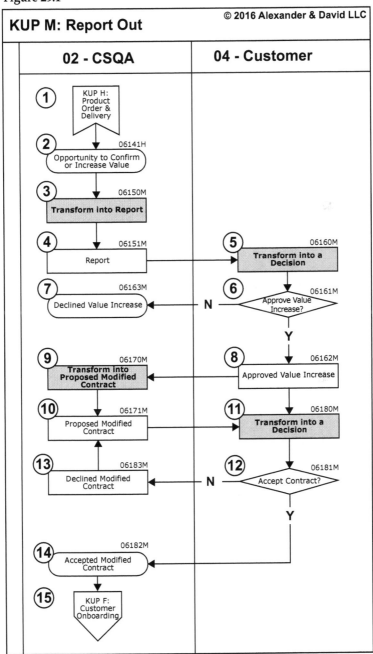

2. *06141H*
   Opportunity to Confirm or Increase Value
   > *Opportunity to confirm or increase value* is a throughput output of KUP H.

3. *06150M*
   Transform Opportunity to Confirm or Increase Value into Report
   > CSQA transforms *an opportunity to confirm or increase value* into a *report.*

4. *06151M*
   Report
   > *Report* is a throughput output of KWP 06150M.

5. *06160M*
   Transform Report into Decision to Approve Value Increase
   > CSQA transforms the *report* into a *decision* to approve value increase.

6. *06161M Approve Value Increase?*
   > The Customer *decides* whether or not to approve the value increase.

7. *06163M*
   Declined Value Increase
   > *Declined value increase* is a problem output of KWP 06160M.

8. *06162M*
   Approved Value Increase
   > *Approved value increase* is a throughput output of KWP 06160M.

9. *06170M*
   Transform Current Contract into Proposed Modified Contract
   > CSQA transforms an *approved value increase* into a *proposed modified contract.*

10. *06171M*
Proposed Modified Contract
Proposed modified contract is a throughput output of KWP 06170M.

11. *06180M*
Transform Proposed Modified Contract into Decision to Accept Contract
CSQA transforms a *proposed modified contract* into a *decision to accept contract*.

12. *06181M*
Accept Contract?
Customer decides whether or not to *accept contract*.

13. *06183M*
Declined Modified Contract
Declined modified contract is a problem output of KWP 06180M.

14. *06182M*
Accepted Modified Contract
Accepted modified contract is a throughput output of KWP 06180M.

15. *KUP F: Customer Onboarding.*
KUP F is a downstream KUP that receives the accepted modified contract KUP M.

Part 5
Implementing Mission Simple

30
Implementing Mission Simple

OVERVIEW

There are two approaches to implementing Mission Simple: 1) do it yourself; or 2) outsource it. The approach you choose will depend on the resources you have available. If you have an internal quality team, then doing it yourself is feasible. If you do not have an internal quality team, then we strongly recommend you outsource it. The decision you make will determine speed to value and sustainability.

If you choose to perform this work internally, you will need to have your internal implementation leader Certified in System Design (Figure 30.1). If you choose to outsource, your external resource must be certified in Advanced System Design (Figure 30.1) and be a licensed *Mission Simple Partner*. Of course, there is nothing preventing you from employing the principles of Mission Simple without adhering to these criteria, however, there is greater risk of failing to achieve sustainable improvement.

In this chapter, we provide an overview of our recommended implementation process. We have conducted numerous implementations and have sharpened the process to make it as effective as possible.

Figure 30.1

CERTIFIED SYSTEM
DESIGNER (CSD)

ADVANCED SYSTEM
DESIGNER (ASD)

Implementation has three phases:

1. *Training*
2. *Design*
3. *Activation*

TRAINING

In the first phase of implementation, the entire team is trained in Mission Simple. The training consists of book study, group training and one-on-one coaching. The training follows the outline of this book and the book is used as a training text.

- **Principles**
    - *Mission Simple*
    - *Customer-Supplier Relationships*
    - *Universal Business System Design (UBSD)*
    - *Managing the Capabilities of Processes*
    - *Quantitative Alignment*
    - *Quantitative Measurement System Design (MSD)*
- **Fallacies**
    - *Exceptional Effort*
    - *Exceeding Expectations*
    - *Managing by Accountability*

- ***Key Work Systems & Key Work Processes***
  - *Leadership*
  - *Sales*
  - *CSQA*
  - *Research & Development (R&D)*
  - *Business System Control (BSC)*
  - *Supplier*
  - *Production System*
- ***Key UBSD Processes***
  - *Sales Business Plan*
  - *R&D Business Plan*
  - *Work System Business Plan*
  - *New Customer Opportunity*
  - *New Customer Engagement*
  - *Customer Onboarding*
  - *Supplier Selection*
  - *Product Order & Delivery*
  - *Problem Response Plan*
  - *New Process or Redesign*
  - *CCRP*
  - *Service Recovery*
  - *Report Out*

The best results are achieved when training is completed in seven weeks with two, two-hour sessions each week for each team. Teams should comprise no more than fifteen participants. Total group training time ranges from 50-60 hours. One-on-one coaching time ranges from 15-30 hours.

Formal course studies for certification in Certified System Design (CSD) and Advanced System Design (ASD) are available. We recommend at least one member of the organization receive CSD certification. If you intend to implement Mission Simple yourself, then we strongly urge you to have your implementation leader become certified.

DESIGN

In the second phase of implementation, the team designs the *future state*. Strategic Planning is not called out as part of this phase, because we assume it has already been done and Mission/Vision/Values, strategic objectives, and quantitative Key Performance Indicators all exist. If these items do not exist, then Strategic Planning should be added to this work.

- ***Map Current State*** - Document how "work" flows through the current business system.

- ***Quantitative Alignment*** - Quantify objectives from Executive Stakeholder and Customers and follow Quantitative Alignment process outlined in *Chapter 5: Quantitative Alignment* (page 45). Execute KUP's outlined in chapters 17-19.

- ***Map Future State*** - Use UBSD framework to create future state. Map KUP's and sub-processes outlined in chapters 20-24, and 26-28.

- ***MSD*** - Follow process outlined in *Chapter 6: Measurement System Design* (page 51) to build a future state MSD.

- ***Response Plan*** - Create a Production System response plan based on MSD and outlined in *Chapter 25: Response Plan* (page 197).

This work also achieves the best results when completed in seven weeks with two, two-hour sessions each week for each team. Teams should comprise no more than fifteen participants. Total work session time ranges from 50-60 hours. One-on-one coaching time ranges from 15-30 hours.

ACTIVATION

In the third phase of implementation, the team activates the UBSD and its *future state*.

- ***Activation Plan Design***
- ***Table-Top***
- ***Audit/Troubleshooting***

The first two steps for this work are completed in two, two-hour sessions and one full-day session. The full-day session brings all the team members together for a table-top walk through. Audit/ Troubleshooting is completed once every month for a period of six months and requires one to two days each month. Following the initial Audit/Troubleshooting work, the frequency of this work can be reduced to once every two months. This work must be completed by your internal leader Certified in System Design (CSD) or by an external resource certified in Advanced System Design (ASD) and licensed as a *Mission Simple Partner*.

31
Epilogue

Mission Simple is a multi-dimensional approach to business performance excellence and includes three principles:

1. Customer-Supplier Relationships

2. Decision-Maker/Problem-Solver

3. Culture & Risk

Businesses can become sustainable in a measurable way by mastering these three core dimensions. This series is about more than Lean, Six Sigma, Baldrige or any other single methodology. While the skilled reader has no doubt picked up on these synergies, these established disciplines are more about influences and less about inspirations.

The material in this book covers the first dimension of the Mission Simple approach to business performance excellence. The Universal Business System Design (UBSD) is a very comprehensive tool that guides people and organizations through the challenging task of aligning their business model to optimize relationships on both the customer and the supplier side.

There is no doubt that some of the concepts in this book are controversial, and may even rub some people the wrong way, but that is okay. Once the reader applies the concepts of this book, those controversies will prove themselves out, and the resulting benefits to the organization will make the point better than our writing ever could.

Exceptional effort is a thing of the past. It is not sustainable and leads to burn-out. It has a secondary impact that organizations seldom realize or understand: inequity of work. Exceptional effort makes some of the workforce believe they are indispensable and others think they are not good at what they do. This will have a negative impact on the culture of the organization, and the disparities seldom, if ever, lead to high function.

Exceeding expectations is another area that will consume an organization's resources without return. It is less about customer satisfaction and more about sustaining to meet the expectations of more customers. This is sometimes hard to grasp for organizations that have become indoctrinated into believing that only those who exceed expectations can succeed. While everyone likes to be delighted by the services and products they receive, we believe that people are willing to pay for consistency and value. Exceeding this expectation will cost businesses money, impede their ability to serve a larger customer base, and essentially eat into their margin.

Managing by accountability is another area where leadership is basically giving up on the idea that people can find the value of the work in the work itself. To be clear, accountability in the way we describe in Mission Simple Book I, is about holding people accountable to perform ineffective processes. This leads to further disparity in the workforce, but instead of the workforce-versus-workforce disparity as identified in the fallacy of exceptional effort, it leads to disparity between the workforce and the management of an organization. Do not mistake this definition of accountability with that of stewardship or accounting. The definition of accountability we describe here has everything to do with the reward and reprimand systems that have swept business in America, and replaces that with one of high value work done by all.

Later in this series we will publish *Mission Simple Book II: Decision-Maker/Problem-Solver*, which will describe the dysfunction of trying to solve problems by making decisions and by trying to make decisions by solving problems. It is a common business dysfunction we have seen in virtually every business with which we have ever had a relationship. The foundation of the dysfunction is that people get promoted through their work system because they prove themselves to be good problem solvers, but seldom do they learn how to effectively make decisions. They spend their time in leadership roles, all the way to the top tier, trying to solve problems. There is a purposeful line that we will demonstrate, and how to transition people from front-line problem solvers to world class decision-makers.

In *Mission Simple Book III: Culture & Risk*, we will describe how culture and risk are related, and how to move a culture to solidify an organization's position. When combined with sound decision-making and problem solving, and a sustainable business system design, a business can assume enormous risk, and advance as a truly exceptionally performing entity.

A future view into our continuing work on developing the very highest-performing organizations includes our second book series: *Mission Critical*, which will walk organizations through the process of continually identifying and improving their most critical needs. Identifying the most important thing advances an organization above its current capabilities. Achieving best-in-market results is the objective of this series.

Every business has the ability to thrive. When relationships between customers and suppliers are managed to bring value, it builds sustainability that delivers the organization's mission into the future. This is where the sweet spot of business resides. Complex does not have to be complicated. That is the point of Mission Simple. There is no doubt that the methodology proposed in this series is complex, but it is doable. It is achievable, and most of all, it is executable. We look forward to a thousand successes in helping businesses of all kinds begin on their road to sustainability by following these principles and becoming truly exceptional organizations.

More value, less waste, more harmony, more equity, more order, and more margin!! Enjoy the journey!!

Marcus A. Oksa, MS, RCP

Peshtigo, Wisconsin

April 2016

Glossary

A

Advanced System Designer (ASD) - An accreditation certifying that an individual has successfully completed the *Advanced System Design* curriculum and testing.

B

Business System - A business system is the highest level system and coordinates an organization's multiple Key Work Systems to deliver value to the Executive Stakeholders and the Customers. The Universal Business System Design (UBSD) is a business system.

Business System Control (BSC) - Business System Control (BSC) is the seventh Key Work System in the UBSD. BSC transforms Customer requirements from CSQA and business requirements from Leadership into specifications to Suppliers and the Production System.

C

Capable Process - A capable process describes a stable process whose capabilities are capable of meeting Customer requirements.

Capacity - Capacity describes the volume of work the Production System can accept with current processes and resources.

Carrots and Sticks - Incentives and penalties employed to manage ineffective processes.

CCRP - The Communication and

Conflict Resolution Plan (CCRP) defines how CSQA will proactively respond to a Production System process that is not meeting requirements (a problem) and communicate the gap to the Customer while seeking a course of action to meet requirements.

Certified System Designer (CSD) - An accreditation certifying that an individual has successfully completed the *Certified System Design* curriculum and testing.

Consumer - The Consumer is the recipient of the product or services being produced by the Production System. The Consumer can be the Customer; however, the Consumer is not always the Customer. The difference between the Consumer and the Customer is that the Customer is always the payer, whereas the Consumer is not always the payer for the Product or Service.

CSQA - CSQA is the Customer's gateway to the Work System and the value it can deliver. CSQA is responsible for transforming the Customers' quantitative Customer objectives into quantitative Customer requirements and aligning them with the Work System's process capabilities. CSQA protects the Work System from the waste created when the Customer enters the Work System in an attempt manage outcomes. CSQA achieves this through Quantitative Alignment with the Customer which confirms that the Work System's process capabilities are capable of meeting the Customer's requirements; and

through R&D which redesigns any processes that are incapable of meeting Customer requirements.

Culture & Risk - The third principle of Mission Simple. Defines the critical relationship between culture and risk and the waste that occurs when a dysfunctional culture creates an ineffective approach to risk jeopardizing the sustainability of the organization.

Current State - Describes the *current* business and/or Work System design and functionality.

Customer - The Customer is defined as the payer for a specific value to be delivered by the Work System. The Customer defines the value they require via quantitative Customer objectives.

Customer-Supplier Relationships - The rules of Customer-Supplier Relationships were first introduced by Toyota's Kaoru Ishikawa and have been widely adopted with proven success. Ishikawa's rules are: 1) the Customer must provide clear and sufficient requirements to the Supplier; and 2) the Supplier must deliver adequate value to meet the requirements of the Customer. Mission Simple expands the application of these rules to include the entire business system and the relationships within and throughout the organization. We differentiate the internal relationships from the external relationships in the following way: External Customers and Suppliers have big "C" and big "S" when we describe them; and internal customer and suppliers have little "c" and little "s" when we describe them.

D

Decision-Maker/Problem-Solver - The second principle of Mission Simple. Defines the common dysfunction and waste created when the the wrong roles are making decisions or solving problems for the wrong reasons.

E

Effective - Effective describes a process, a linked series of processes, or a system that deliver the most value, in the shortest time, at the lowest cost.

Exceeding Expectations - To produce and deliver more product or services than the Customer requires without receiving additional payment.

Exceptional Business Performance - Exceptional business performance describes the state in which an organization is sustainably delivering the most value, in the shortest time, for the lowest cost.

Exceptional Effort - Exceptional effort describes the effort necessary to manage a process with a wide range of variation to consistently achieve required results.

Executive Stakeholder - The Executive Stakeholders are the organization's owners or owners' representatives (i.e. Board Members and C-Suite executives). They are responsible for making

strategic decisions about the Work System; decisions about how to protect and capitalize on the capabilities of the Work System in order to be effective and sustainable in the organization's markets. The are also responsible for making strategic decisions about what should be procured or produced externally to ensure their Work System is effective and sustainable.

F

FTE - Full-time-equivalent is the percent of an employee's full-time hours the employee spends performing work. (1.0 FTE is generally accepted as 2080 hours per year.)

Future State - Describes the *future* business and/or Work System design and functionality.

I

Influencer - Influencers are independent organizations, NGO's or government agencies that impose laws, regulations, or public relations pressure on the Executive Stakeholders in an effort to influence the priorities the Executive Stakeholders set for the organization. In the case of regulatory agencies, they can exert significant influence (e.g. Healthcare, Oil and Gas, Power, etc.)

Input - Input is whatever must be supplied to a process in order for the process to be effective. Input is also supply.

Inventory - All the cash invested to purchase the resources, materials and parts the business system intends to sell (Source: *The Goal*, Eliyahu M. Goldratt and Jeff Cox).

Ishikawa, Kaoru - While at Toyota, Ishikawa introduced the principles of Customer-Supplier Relationships. Author of *What is Total Quality Control? The Japanese Way.*

K

Key Performance Indicators (KPI's) - KPI's are the quantitative measures that define whether or not strategic objectives are being met.

Key UBSD Process - Key UBSD Processes (KUP's) are "inter" processes that reside between multiple Key Work Systems linking them to produce specific deliverables or value to the Customer.

Key Work Processes - Within each Key Work System are one or more Key Work Processes (KWP's). KWP's are "intra" processes and reside solely "within" a single KWS. Collectively, the KWP's produce the output of the KWS.

Key Work System - A Key Work System coordinates Key Work Processes to deliver value to the Customer.

L

Leadership - Leadership is positioned between the Executive Stakeholder and the Work System and is responsible for transforming the Executive Stakeholders' business objectives (expressed quantitatively as Key Performance Indicators or KPI's) into quantitative business requirements and then aligning them with the Work System's process capabilities. If the processes are capable of meeting the requirements, then Leadership accepts them and forwards them to Business System Control, R&D, and Sales. If not, Leadership forwards them to R&D for redesign.

Local Optimization - Local Optimization occurs when individual Key Work Systems solve their own problems independent of the business system. This is the most common method problems are resolved in most organizations but it is also the primary creator of system waste. Business System Optimization is a more effective method of resolving problems because it reduces waste rather than creating waste.

M

Managing by Accountability - The current, widely-accepted belief that leaders and managers can achieve required results by holding workers accountable and is built on the false belief that the value of a worker is defined by the worker's ability to manage unstable, incapable processes with wide variation. And rather than fix the processes, to use carrots and sticks to drive the worker.

Managing the Capabilities of People - Managing the Capabilities of People defines the method of achieving business performance results by managing the capabilities of people. This is the most commonly used approach and is ineffective, creating significant waste and jeopardizing the sustainability of organizations. It is ineffective because the capabilities of people have wide variation requiring the manual manipulation of managers in order for work to meet requirements.

Managing the Capabilities of Processes - Managing the Capabilities of Processes defines the method of achieving business performance results by managing the capabilities of processes (rather than people). This approach eliminates the dependence on the exceptional few and provides a way for all workers to add more value. The purpose of managing the capabilities of processes is to narrow the range of variation such that manual manipulation is no longer required.

Market - The Market is defined as *all* of the organization's current and prospective Customers.

Measurement System Design - Measurement System Design (MSD) defines the engine that drives Quantitative Alignment (see Chapter 5: Quantitative Alignment). The MSD focuses on a small set of key quantitative measures, designs and implements data collection processes, and provides an effective distribution platform to UBSD team members. The MSD replaces qualitative measures with quantitative measures (see Chapter 4: Managing the Capabilities of Process). Quantitative measures are objective, and qualitative measures are subjective. The weakness of qualitative measures is they allow for a wide range of variation. Variation creates waste and waste increases costs and slows throughput. To reduce variation, the MSD uses quantitative measures to align the priorities of the Executive Stakeholders and Customers with the process capabilities of the Suppliers and the Work System.

Mission Simple - Mission Simple provides organizations with a highly effective methodology for achieving Performance Excellence[1.1] through exceptional business performance. Exceptional business performance describes the state in which an organization is sustainably delivering the most value, in the shortest time, for the lowest cost. Mission Simple introduces three qualitative core principles: 1) Customer/Supplier Relationships; 2) Decision-Makers/Problem-Solver; and 3) Culture & Risk. Mission Simple supports its qualitative core principles with a continuous quantitative performance measurement cycle: Measure, Diagnose, Resolve. Mission Simple's unique integration of the qualitative and quantitative ignites exceptional business performance.

N

Narrow Variation - Narrow variation describes a process whose capabilities have small deviation from the mean. The smaller the deviation, the more frequently the process delivers the mean result, increasing value to the Customer and reducing waste. A process with narrow variation is described as being *stable*.

Non-Value Add but Required (NVR) - (muda type 1) NVR describes roles and processes whose outputs do not add value to the Customer but are required to support the organization (e.g. Billing, Payroll, HR, Legal, etc.)

O

Objective - What we want to accomplish with the help of the Work System. Only two of the four players in the business system set objectives for the Work System: The Executive Stakeholders and the Customers. The Executive Stakeholders are responsible for making strategic decisions about how to protect and capitalize on the capabilities of the Work System in order to be effective and sustainable in the organization's markets; and decisions about what should be procured or produced externally to ensure the Work System is effective and sustainable. This work is done during strategic planning. The Executive Stakeholder's objectives are strategic decisions expressed quantitatively as a Key Performance Indicator or KPI which is a measure used by the Executive Stakeholder to determine if their Work System is progressing toward the objective. KPI's represent the Executive Stakeholder's most important metrics for the Work System and, as such, receive the greatest support and funding.

Operational Expenses - All the cash spent by the business system in order to turn inventory into sales (Source: *The Goal*, Eliyahu M. Goldratt and Jeff Cox).

Output - Output is the product or service produced by a process. All value add processes feature outputs with higher value than inputs.

P

Performance Excellence - The term "performance excellence" refers to an integrated approach to organizational performance management that results in (1) delivery of ever-improving value to customers and stakeholders, contributing to organizational sustainability; (2) improvement of overall organizational effectiveness and capabilities; and (3) organizational and personal learning. The Baldrige Criteria for Performance Excellence provide a framework and an assessment tool for understanding organizational strengths and opportunities for improvement and thus for guiding planning efforts. (Source: Baldrige21.com)

Process Capabilities - Process capabilities define the range of results a process produces over time. Process capabilities are documented in a control chart.

Problem - A problem is defined as a process with defined capabilities that begins producing multiple results outside of its established control limits. For example, let's say the "time-to-finish" capabilities for a process ranges from five to fifteen minutes. A single result outside of that range is not a problem. However, a number of results outside of that range indicates a problem.

Problem Alert - A problem alert is a notification to the Production System and CSQA that a process is experiencing a problem.

Problem Output - A problem output is a barrier to effective throughput and requires a remedy to restore effective throughput.

Problem Resolved - A problem resolved defines a process that has returned to producing results within established control limits.

Problem Unresolved - A problem unresolved defines a process that continues to produce multiple results beyond established control limits.

Process - One or more linked activities that transform inputs into higher value outputs.

Process Capabilities - Process capabilities describe the results a process is capable of producing repeatedly over time without manual manipulation.

Production System - The Production System is where the product is produced or the service is delivered. It consists of one or more processes that transform supplies and Production System capacity into finished products or services delivered to the Consumer.

Q

Quantitative Alignment - Quantitative Alignment aligns the organization's four core constituents quantitatively: Executive Stakeholders, Customers, Suppliers and the Work System. Quantitative Alignment eliminates the wide variation associated with qualitative alignment and provides the Executive Stakeholders and Customers with a higher degree of assurance that the Work System will meet their objectives.

R

Repeatable - The range of process variation is consistent when the process is performed by the same individual over time.

Reproducible - The range of process variation is consistent when the process is performed by different individuals over time.

Requirement - The work the Work System must be do. Requirements define the required outputs of the Work System to meet the objectives (i.e. what the Work System must produce in order to meet objectives). Requirements are defined in terms of quantity, time, quality, and cost. Requirements identify the Work System processes that must be followed in order to meet the objectives of both the Executive Stakeholders and the Customers. If you know what your processes must produce quantitatively, and you know your process capabilities, you can determine which combination of processes will produce results that meet requirements and meet the objectives.

Research & Development (R&D) - R&D transforms incapable processes (processes whose current capabilities do not meet Customer requirements) into capable processes; and designs new processes to meet Customer requirements today and in the future.

Response Plan - A Response Plan is a a set of instructions for the Production System directing appropriate response to processes that are not meeting pre-defined capabilities. A response plan defines the acceptable performance limits for a process and the actions to implement when a process is performing outside of these limits.

S

Sales - Sales delivers new Customers to CSQA to meet the quantitative business requirements of Leadership.

Service Recovery - Service Recovery is a Key UBSD Process (KUP) employed when the Work System processes cannot meet Customer requirements. It provides the Customer with one or more external alternatives capable of meeting requirements in order to maintain a relationship in good standing with the Customer.

Simple Six - The Simple Six™ tells us: 1) Are we making money? and 2) Are we meeting Customer requirements for quality, volume, time, and cost? Includes revenue, FTE, volume, time-to-start, time-to-finish, and cost.

Specification - The resources and capacity required to perform the work that must be done. Specifications define the Supplier resources, materials or parts, and the Work System process capacity required to meet Requirements. (Usually defined as quantity, time and cost.)

Stable - The range of process variation is both narrow and consistent over time.

Supplier - The Supplier delivers the resources, materials or parts to the Production System to meet BSC specifications.

Supply - Supply is the resources, materials or parts delivered by the Supplier to the Production System. Supply is also the input of a process.

Sustainable - Sustainable describes a process, a linked series of processes, or a system that is stable, repeatable and reproducible.

Swim Lane Diagram - A cross-functional swim lane diagram visually distinguishes multiple jobs, roles and responsibilities for cross-functional processes and sub-processes. It establishes boundaries between roles. Swim lanes may be arranged horizontally or vertically.

System - A system coordinates

multiple processes or sub-systems to deliver value to an internal or external customer.

T

Throughput - The rate the business system generates cash through sales (Source: *The Goal*, Eliyahu M. Goldratt and Jeff Cox).

Throughput Output - A throughput output is an output that contributes to effective business system throughput.

Time to Finish - The quantitative measure of the duration of time from the time *when work begins* to the time *when value is delivered* to the Customer.

Time to Start - The quantitative measure of the duration of time from the time *when work is requested* by the Customer to *when work begins*.

U

Universal Business System Design - The Universal Business System Design (UBSD) provides the framework to support the principle of Customer-Supplier Relationships. The UBSD defines the relationships and work flow between the key roles in the business system and supports the quantitative alignment between the organization's four core constituents: Executive Stakeholders, Customers, Suppliers and the Work System.

V

Value-Added (VA) - The phrase used to describe a process that adds value to the Customer (a process that produces an output the Customer is willing to pay for).

Variation - Describes the distance between control limits on a process control chart, or the range of process results from high to low for any given result. Wide variation is unstable and creates waste; narrow variation is stable and reduces waste.

W

Waste - Waste describes activities that do not add value to the Customer.

Wide Variation - Wide variation describes a process whose capabilities have large deviation from the mean. The larger the deviation, the less frequently the process delivers the mean result, decreasing value to the Customer and increasing waste. A process with wide variation is described as being *unstable*.

Work Flow - Describes how work is pulled through the Work System to meet Customer requirements.

Work System - The Work System is the second level system and coordinates the Supplier and Production System Key Work Systems to deliver value to the Customer.

Marcus A. Oksa, MS, RCP

Marcus A. Oksa, MS, RCP, is a Lean Six Sigma Black Belt and has been a Baldrige facilitator and coach for multiple organizations. Marcus has served as President of the Wisconsin Medical Group Management Association (WMGMA) and is an Adjunct Faculty member at Bellin College and Marian University. Marcus is also a U.S. Army Gulf War veteran and Bronze Star recipient.

Throughout his 20-year career Marcus has developed new, innovative methodologies for problem identification, waste reduction, strategic and tactical definition, and process and organizational mapping. His techniques have been successfully applied in every department of a healthcare system with remarkable success. In addition to the anticipated outcomes of Lean Six Sigma cost and variation reduction, his projects have improved morale, built cohesive work groups, and empowered people to appreciate their work.

Marcus lives with his wife Linda and children in Peshtigo, Wisconsin.

Michael D. Wentworth, ASD

Michael D. Wentworth, ASD, has a 35-year career consulting in sales, marketing, advertising and market research for for-profit and non-profit organizations in virtually every market sector from start-ups to Fortune 500 companies including private equity firms. His clients have included Sears, National Car Rental, 3M, Medtronic, HB Fuller, Brady Corporation, Tennant, Bellin Health, Subway Foods, Rockwell Automation, Marshfield Clinics, Yale New Haven Health System, US Captioning, Performa Inc., Pathmakers Inc., MCI, LMG Presses, and more.

During his career, Michael has developed innovative methods in sales, competitive intelligence and qualitative research.

Michael lives in Kaukauna, Wisconsin with his wife Laurie.